Barcode in Back

MW01122462

The Vikings
of Helgeland

Henrik Ibsen

Translated by William Archer

HUMBER LIBRARIES LAKESHORE CAMPUS
3199 Lakeshore Blvd West
TORONTO, ON.   M8V 1K8

THE VIKINGS OF HELGELAND. (1858.)

CHARACTERS.

ORNULF OF THE FIORDS, an Icelandic Chieftain.
SIGURD THE STRONG, a Sea-King.
GUNNAR HEADMAN, [1] a rich yeoman of Helgeland.
DAGNY, Ornulf's daughter.
HIORDIS, his foster-daughter.
KARE THE PEASANT, a Helgeland-man.
EGIL, Gunnar's son, four years old.
ORNULF'S SIX OLDER SONS.
ORNULF'S AND SIGURD'S MEN.
Guests, house-carls, serving-maids, outlaws, etc.

The action takes place in the time of Erik Blood-axe (about A. D. 933) at, and in the neighbourhood of, Gunnar's house on the island of Helgeland, in the north of Norway.

[PRONUNCIATION OF NAMES.

—Helgeland=Helgheland;
Ornulf=Ornoolf;
Sigurd=Sigoord;
Gunnar=Goonar;
Thorolf=Toorolf;
Hiordis=Yordeess;
Kare=Koare [e, umlaut];
Egil=Ayghil.
The letter o [umlaut] as in German.]

[1] Failing to find a better equivalent for the Norwegian "Herse, " I have used the word "Headman" wherever it seemed necessary to give Gunnar a title or designation. He is generally spoken of as "Gunnar Herse" in the Norwegian text; but where it could be done without inconvenience, the designation has here been omitted.

THE VIKINGS OF HELGELAND.

PLAY IN FOUR ACTS.

ACT FIRST.

(A rocky coast, running precipitously down to the sea at the back. To the left, a boat-house; to the right, rocks and pine-woods. The masts of two war-ships can be seen down in the cove. Far out to the right, the ocean, dotted with reefs and rocky islands; the sea is running high; it is a stormy snow-grey winter day.)

(SIGURD comes up from the ships; he is clad in a white tunic with a silver belt, a blue cloak, cross-gartered hose, untanned shoes, and a steel cap; at his side hangs a short sword. ORNULF comes in sight immediately afterwards, up among the rocks, clad in a dark lamb-skin tunic with a breastplate and greaves, woollen stockings, and untanned shoes; over his shoulders he has a cloak of brown frieze, with the hood drawn over his steel cap, so that his face is partly hidden. He is very tall, and massively built, with a long white beard, but somewhat bowed by age; his weapons are a round shield, sword, and spear.

SIGURD (enters first, looks around, sees the boat-shed, goes quickly up to it, and tries to burst open the door.)

ORNULF (appears among the rocks, starts on seeing SIGURD, seems to recognise him, descends and cries:) Give place, Viking!

SIGURD (turns, lays his hand on his sword, and answers:) 'Twere the first time if I did!

ORNULF. Thou shalt and must! I have need of the shelter for my stiff-frozen men.

SIGURD. Then must outlaws be highly prized in Helgeland!

ORNULF. Dearly shalt thou aby that word!

SIGURD. Now will it go ill with thee, old man!

(ORNULF rushes upon him; SIGURD defends himself.) (DAGNY and some of SIGURD'S men come up from the strand; Ornulf's six sons appear on the rocks to the right.)

DAGNY (who is a little in front, clad in a red kirtle, blue cloak, and fur hood, calls down to the ships:) Up, all Sigurd's men! My husband is fighting with a stranger!

ORNULF'S SONS. Help for Ornulf! (They descend.)

SIGURD (to his men). Hold! I can master him alone!

ORNULF (to his sons). Let me fight in peace! (Rushes in upon SIGURD.) I will see thy blood!

SIGURD. First see thine own! (Wounds him in the arm so that his spear falls.)

ORNULF. A stout stroke, Viking!
      Swift the sword thou swingest,
      keen thy blows and biting;
      Sigurd's self, the Stalwart,
      stood before thee shame-struck.

SIGURD (smiling). Then were his shame his glory!

ORNULF'S SONS (with a cry of wonder). Sigurd himself! Sigurd the Strong!

ORNULF. But sharper was thy stroke that night thou didst bear away Dagny, my daughter. (Casts his hood back.)

SIGURD AND HIS MEN. Ornulf of the Fiords!

DAGNY (glad, yet uneasy). My father and my brothers!

SIGURD. Stand thou behind me.

ORNULF. Nay, no need. (Approaching SIGURD.) I knew thy face as soon as I was ware of thee, and therefore I stirred the strife; I was fain to prove the fame that tells of thee as the stoutest man of his hands in Norway. Henceforth let peace be between us.

SIGURD. Best if so it could be.

ORNULF. Here is my hand. Thou art a warrior indeed; stouter strokes than these has old Ornulf never given or taken.

SIGURD (seizes his outstretched hand). Let them be the last strokes given and taken between us two; and do thou thyself adjudge the matter between us. Art thou willing?

ORNULF. That am I, and straightway shall the quarrel be healed. (To the others.) Be the matter, then, known to all. Five winters ago came Sigurd and Gunnar Headman as vikings to Iceland; they lay in harbour close under my homestead. Then Gunnar, by force and craft, carried away my foster-daughter, Hiordis; but thou, Sigurd, didst take Dagny, my own child, and sailed with her over the sea. For that thou art now doomed to pay three hundred pieces of silver, and thereby shall thy misdeed be atoned.

SIGURD. Fair is thy judgment, Ornulf; the three hundred pieces will I pay, and add thereto a silken cloak fringed with gold. It is a gift from King AEthelstan of England, and better has no Icelander yet borne.

DAGNY. So be it, my brave husband; and my father, I thank thee. Now at last is my mind at ease.

(She presses her father's and brothers' hands, and talks low to them.)

ORNULF. Then thus stands the treaty between us; and from this day shall Dagny be to the full as honourably regarded as though she had been lawfully betrothed to thee, with the good will of her kin.

SIGURD. And in me canst thou trust, as in one of thine own blood.

ORNULF. That doubt I not; and see! I will forthwith prove thy friendship.

SIGURD. Ready shalt thou find me; say, what dost thou crave?

ORNULF. Thy help in rede and deed. I have sailed hither to Helgeland to seek out Gunnar Headman and draw him to reckoning for the carrying away of Hiordis.

SIGURD (surprised). Gunnar!

DAGNY (in the same tone). And Hiordis—where are they?

ORNULF. In Gunnar's homestead, I ween.

SIGURD. And it is— —?

ORNULF. Not many bow-shots hence; did ye not know?

SIGURD (with suppressed emotion). No, truly. Small tidings have I had of Gunnar since we sailed from Iceland together. I have wandered far and wide and served many outland kings, while Gunnar sat at home. Hither we drive at day-dawn before the storm; I knew, indeed, that Gunnar's homestead lay here in the north, but——

DAGNY (to ORNULF). So *that* errand has brought thee hither?

ORNULF. That and no other. (To SIGURD.) Our meeting is the work of the Mighty Ones above; they willed it so. Had I wished to find thee, little knew I where to seek.

SIGURD (thoughtfully). True, true! —But concerning Gunnar—tell me, Ornulf, art thou minded to go sharply to work, with all thy might, be it for good or ill?

ORNULF. That must I. Listen, Sigurd, for thus it stands: Last summer I rode to the Council where many honourable men were met. When the Council-days were over, I sat in the hall and drank with the men of my hundred, and the talk fell upon the carrying-away of the women; scornful words they gave me, because I had let that wrong rest unavenged. Then, in my wrath, I swore to sail to Norway, seek out Gunnar, and crave reckoning or revenge, and never again to set foot in Iceland till my claim was made good.

SIGURD. Ay, ay, since so it stands, I see well that if need be the matter must be pressed home.

ORNULF. It must; but I shall not crave over much, and Gunnar has the fame of an honourable man. Glad am I, too, that I set about this quest; the time lay heavy on me in Iceland; out upon the blue waters had I grown old and grey, and I longed to fare forth once again before I— —; well well—Bergthora, my good wife, was dead these many years; my eldest sons sailed on viking-ventures summer by summer; and since Thorolf was growing up— —

DAGNY (gladly). Thorolf is with thee? Where is he?

ORNULF. On board the ship. (Points towards the background, to the right.) Scarce shalt thou know the boy again, so stout and strong and fair has he grown. He will be a mighty warrior, Sigurd; one day he will equal thee.

DAGNY (smiling). I see it is now as ever; Thorolf stands nearest thy heart.

ORNULF. He is the youngest, and like his mother; therefore it is.

SIGURD. But tell me—thy errand to Gunnar—thinkest thou to-day— —?

ORNULF. Rather to-day than to-morrow. Fair amends will content me; if Gunnar says me nay, then must he take what comes.

(KARE THE PEASANT enters hastily from the right; he is clad in a grey frieze cloak and low-brimmed felt hat; he carries in his hand a broken fence-rail.)

KARE. Well met, Vikings!

ORNULF. Vikings are seldom well met.

KARE. If ye be honourable men, ye will grant me refuge among you; Gunnar Headman's house-carls are hunting me to slay me.

ORNULF. Gunnar's?

SIGURD. Then has thou done him some wrong!

KARE. I have done myself right. Our cattle fed together upon an island, hard by the coast; Gunnar's men carried off my best oxen, and one of them flouted me for a thrall. Then bare I arms against him and slew him.

ORNULF. That was a lawful deed.

KARE. But this morning his men came in wrath against me. By good hap I heard of their coming, and fled; but my foemen are on my tracks, and short shrift can I look for at their hands.

SIGURD. Ill can I believe thee, peasant! In bygone days I knew Gunnar as I know myself, and this I wot, that never did he wrong a peaceful man.

KARE. Gunnar has no part in this wrong-doing; he is in the south-land; nay, it is Hiordis his wife— —

DAGNY. Hiordis!

ORNULF (to himself). Ay, ay, 'tis like her!

KARE. I offered Gunnar amends for the thrall, and he was willing; but then came Hiordis, and egged her husband on with scornful words, and hindered the peace. Since then has Gunnar gone to the south, and to-day— —

SIGURD (looking out to the left). Here come wayfarers northward. Is it not— —?

KARE. It is Gunnar himself!

ORNULF. Be of good heart; methinks I can make peace between you.

(GUNNAR HEADMAN, with several men, enters from the left. He is in a brown tunic, cross-gartered hose, a blue mantle, and a broad hat; he has no weapon but a small axe.)

GUNNAR (stops in surprise and uncertainty on seeing the knot of men). Ornulf of the Fiords! Yes, it is— —!

ORNULF. Thou seest aright.

GUNNAR (approaching). Then peace and welcome to thee in my land, if thou come in peace.

ORNULF. If thy will be as mine, there shall be no strife between us.

SIGURD (standing forward). Well met, Gunnar!

GUNNAR (gladly). Sigurd—foster-brother! (Shakes his hand.) Now truly, since thou art here, I know that Ornulf comes in peace. (To ORNULF.) Give me thy hand, greybeard! Thy errand here in the north is lightly guessed: it has to do with Hiordis, thy foster-daughter.

ORNULF. As thou sayest; great wrong was done me when thou didst bear her away from Iceland without my will.

GUNNAR. Thy claim is just; what youth has marred, the man must mend. Long have I looked for thee, Ornulf, for this cause; and if amends content thee, we shall soon be at one.

SIGURD. So deem I too. Ornulf will not press thee hard.

GUNNAR (warmly). Nay, Ornulf, didst thou crave her full worth, all my goods would not suffice.

ORNULF. I shall go by law and usage, be sure of that. But now another matter. (Pointing to KARE.) Seest thou yonder man?

GUNNAR. Kare! (To ORNULF.) Thou knowest, then, that there is a strife between us?

ORNULF. Thy men have stolen his cattle, and theft must be atoned.

GUNNAR. Murder no less; he has slain my thrall.

KARE. Because he flouted me.

GUNNAR. I have offered thee terms of peace.

KARE. But that had Hiordis no mind to, and this morning, whilst thou wert gone, she fell upon me and hunts me now to my death.

GUNNAR (angrily). Is it true what thou sayest? Has she——?

KARE. True, every word.

ORNULF. Therefore the peasant besought me to stand by him, and that will I do.

GUNNAR (after a moment's thought). Honourably hast thou dealt with me, Ornulf; therefore is it fit that I should yield to thy will. Hear then, Kare: I am willing to let the slaying of the thrall and the wrongs done toward thee quit each other.

KARE (gives GUNNAR his hand). It is a good offer; I am content.

ORNULF. And he shall have peace for thee and thine?

GUNNAR. Peace shall he have, here and overall.

SIGURD (pointing to the right). See yonder!

GUNNAR (disturbed). It is Hiordis!

ORNULF. With armed men!

KARE. She is seeking me!

(HIORDIS enters, with a troop of house-carls. She is clad in black, wearing a kirtle, cloak, and hood; the men are armed with swords and axes; she herself carries a light spear.)

HIORDIS (stops on entering). A meeting of many, meseems.

DAGNY (rushes to meet her). Peace and joy to thee, Hiordis!

HIORDIS (coldly). Thanks. It was told me that thou wast not far off. (Comes forward, looking sharply at those assembled.) Gunnar, and—Kare, my foeman—Ornulf and his sons and—— (As she catches sight of SIGURD, she starts almost imperceptibly, is silent a moment, but collects herself and says:) Many I see here who are known to me— but little I know who is best minded towards me.

ORNULF. We are all well-minded towards thee.

HIORDIS. If so be, thou wilt not deny to give Kare into my husband's hands.

ORNULF. There is no need.

GUNNAR. There is peace and friendship between us.

HIORDIS (with suppressed scorn). Friendship? Well well, I know thou art a wise man, Gunnar! Kare has met mighty friends, and well I woth thou deem'st it safest——

GUNNAR. Thy taunts avail not! (With dignity.) Kare is at peace with us!

HIORDIS (restraining herself). Well and good; if thou hast sworn him peace, the vow must be held.

GUNNAR (forcibly, but without anger). It must and it shall.

ORNULF (to HIORDIS). Another pact had been well-nigh made ere thy coming.

HIORDIS (sharply). Between thee and Gunnar.

ORNULF (nods). It had to do with thee.

HIORDIS. Well can I guess what it had to do with; but this I tell thee, foster-father, never shall it be said that Gunnar let himself be cowed because thou camest in arms to the isle. Hadst thou come alone, a single wayfarer, to our hall, the quarrel had more easily been healed.

GUNNAR. Ornulf and his sons come in peace.

HIORDIS. Mayhap; but otherwise will it sound in the mouths of men; and thou thyself, Gunnar, didst show scant trust in the peace yesterday, in sending our son Egil to the southland so soon as it was known that Ornulf's warship lay in the fiord.

SIGURD (to GUNNAR). Didst thou send thy sons to the south?

HIORDIS. Ay, that he might be in safety should Ornulf fall upon us.

ORNULF. Scoff not at that, Hiordis; what Gunnar has done may prove wise in the end, if so be thou hinderest the pact.

HIORDIS. Life must take its chance; come what will, I had liever die than save my life by a shameful pact.

DAGNY. Sigurd makes atonement, and will not be deemed the lesser man for that.

HIORDIS. Sigurd best knows what his own honour can bear.

SIGURD. On that score shall I never need reminding.

HIORDIS. Sigurd has done famous deeds, but the boldest deed of all was Gunnar's, when he slew the white bear that guarded my bower.

GUNNAR (with an embarrassed glance at SIGURD). Nay nay, no more of that!

ORNULF. In truth it was the boldest deed that e'er was seen in Iceland; and therefore — —

SIGURD. The more easily can Gunnar yield, and not be deemed a coward.

HIORDIS. If amends are to be made, amends shall also be craved. Bethink thee, Gunnar, of thy vow!

GUNNAR. That vow was ill bethought; wilt thou hold me to it?

HIORDIS. That will I, if we two are to dwell under one roof after this day. Know then, Ornulf, that if atonement is to be made for the carrying away of thy foster-daughter, thou, too, must atone for the slaying of Jokul my father, and the seizure of his goods and gear.

ORNULF. Jokul was slain in fair fight; [1] thy kinsmen did me a worse wrong when they sent thee to Iceland and entrapped me into adopting[2] thee, unwitting who thou wast.

[1] "I aerling holmgang." The established form of duel in the viking times was to land the combatants on one of the rocky islets or "holms" that stud the Norwegian coast, and there let them fight it out. Hence "holmgang"=duel.

[2] "At knaessette"=to knee-set a child, to take it on one's knee, an irrevocable form of adoption.

HIORDIS. Honour, and now wrong, befell thee in adopting Jokul's daughter.

ORNULF. Nought but strife hast thou brought me, that I know.

HIORDIS. Sterner strife may be at hand, if——

ORNULF. I came not hither to bandy words with women! —Gunnar, hear my last word: art willing to make atonement?

HIORDIS (to GUNNAR). Think of thy vow!

GUNNAR (to ORNULF). Thou hearest, I have sworn a vow, and that must I——

ORNULF (irritated). Enough, enough! Never shall it be said that I made atonement for slaying in fair fight.

HIORDIS (forcibly). Then we bid defiance to thee and thine.

ORNULF (in rising wrath). And who has the right to crave atonement for Jokul? Where are his kinsmen? There is none alive! Where is his lawful avenger?

HIORDIS. That is Gunnar, on my behalf.

ORNULF. Gunnar! Ay, hadst thou been betrothed to him with thy foster-father's good-will, or had he made atonement for carrying thee away, then were he thy father's lawful avenger; but——

DAGNY (apprehensive and imploring). Father, father!

SIGURD (quickly). Do not speak it!

ORNULF (raising his voice). Nay, loudly shall it be spoken! A woman wedded by force has no lawful husband!

GUNNAR (vehemently). Ornulf!

HIORDIS (in a wild outburst). Flouted and shamed! (In a quivering voice.) This—this shalt thou come to rue!

ORNULF (continuing). A woman wedded by force is lawfully no more than a leman! Wilt thou regain thine honour, then must thou——

HIORDIS (controlling herself). Nay, Ornulf, I know better what is fitting. If I am to be held as Gunnar's leman—well and good, then

12

must he win me honour by his deeds—by deeds so mighty that my shame shall be shame no more! And thou, Ornulf, beware! Here our ways part, and from this day I shall make war upon thee and thine whensoever and wheresoever it may be; thou shalt know no safety, thou, or any whom thou—— (Looking fiercely at KARE.) Kare! Ornulf has stood thy friend, forsooth, and there is peace between us; but I counsel thee not to seek thy home yet awhile; the man thou slewest has many avengers, and it well might befall—— See, I have shown thee the danger; thou must e'en take what follows. Come, Gunnar, we must gird ourselves for the fight. A famous deed didst thou achieve in Iceland, but greater deeds must here be done, if thou wouldst not have thy— thy leman shrink with shame from thee and from herself!

GUNNAR. Curb thyself, Hiordis; it is unseemly to bear thee thus.

DAGNY (imploringly). Stay, foster-sister—stay; I will appease my father.

HIORDIS (without listening to her). Homewards, homewards! Who could have foretold me that I should wear out my life as a worthless leman? But if I am to bear this life of shame, ay, even a single day longer, then must my husband do such a deed—such a deed as shall make his name more famous than all other names of men.

(Goes out to the right.)

GUNNAR (softly). Sigurd, this thou must promise me, that we shall have speech together ere thou leave the land.

(Goes out with his men to the right.) (The storm has meanwhile ceased; the mid-day sun is now visible, like a red disc, low upon the rim of the sea.)

ORNULF (threateningly). Dearly shalt thou aby this day's work, foster-daughter!

DAGNY. Father, father! Surely thou wilt not harm her!

ORNULF. Let me be! Now, Sigurd, now can no amends avail between Gunnar and me.

SIGURD. What thinkest thou to do?

ORNULF. That I know not; but far and wide shall the tale be told how Ornulf of the Fiords came to Gunnar's hall.

SIGURD (with quiet determination). That may be; but this I tell thee, Ornulf, that thou shalt never bear arms against him so long as I am alive.

ORNULF. So, so! And what if it be my will to?

SIGURD. It shall not be—let thy will be never so strong.

ORNULF (angrily). Go then; join thou with my foes; I can match the twain of you!

SIGURD. Hear me out, Ornulf; the day shall never dawn that shall see thee and me at strife. There is honourable peace between us, Dagny is dearer to me than weapons or gold, and never shall I forget that thou art her nearest kinsman.

ORNULF. There I know thee again, brave Sigurd!

SIGURD. But Gunnar is my foster-brother; faith and friendship have we sworn each other. Both in war and peace have we faced fortune together, and of all men he is dearest to me. Stout though he be, he loves not war; —but as for me, ye know, all of you, that I shrink not from strife; yet here I stand forth, Ornulf, and pray for peace on Gunnar's behalf. Let me have my will!

ORNULF. I cannot; I should be a scoff to all brave men, were I to fare empty-handed back to Iceland.

SIGURD. Empty-handed shalt thou not fare. Here in the cove my two long-ships are lying, with all the wealth I have won in my viking- ventures. There are many costly gifts from outland kings, good weapons by the chestful, and other priceless chattels. Take thou one of the ships; choose which thou wilt, and it shall be thine with all it contains—be that the atonement for Hiordis, and let Gunnar be at peace.

ORNULF. Brave Sigurd, wilt thou do this for Gunnar?

SIGURD. For a faithful friend, no man can do too much.

ORNULF. Give half thy goods and gear!

SIGURD (urgently). Take the whole, take both my ships, take all that is mine, and let me fare with thee to Iceland as the poorest man in thy train. What I give, I can win once more; but if thou and Gunnar come to strife, I shall never see a glad day again. Now Ornulf, thy answer?

ORNULF (reflecting). Two good long-ships, weapons and other chattels —too much gear can no man have; but— — (vehemently) no, no! — Hiordis has threatened me; I will not! It were shameful for me to take thy goods!

SIGURD. Yet listen— —

ORNULF. No, I say! I must fight my own battle, be my fortune what it may.

KARE (approaching). Right friendly is Sigurd's rede, but if thou wilt indeed fight thine own battle with all thy might, I can counsel thee better. Dream not of atonement so long as Hiordis has aught to say; but revenge can be thine if thou wilt hearken to me.

ORNULF. Revenge? What dost thou counsel?

SIGURD. Evil, I can well see.

DAGNY (to ORNULF). Oh, do not hear him!

KARE. Hiordis has declared me an outlaw; with cunning will she seek to take my life; do thou swear to see me scatheless, and this night will I burn Gunnar's hall and all within it. Is that to thy mind?

SIGURD. Dastard!

ORNULF (quietly). To my mind? Knowest thou, Kare, what were more to my mind? (In a voice of thunder.) To hew off thy nose and ears, thou vile thrall. Little dost thou know old Ornulf if thou thinkest to have his help in such a deed of shame!

KARE (who has shrunk backwards). If thou fall not upon Gunnar he will surely fall upon thee.

ORNULF. Have I not weapons, and strength to wield them?

SIGURD (to KARE). And now away with thee! Thy presence is a shame to honourable men!

KARE (going off). Well well, I must shield myself as best I can. But this I tell you: if ye think to deal gently with Hiordis, ye will come to rue it; I know her—and I know where to strike her sorest!

(Goes down towards the shore.)

DAGNY. He is plotting revenge. Sigurd, it must be hindered!

ORNULF (with annoyance). Nay, let him do as he will; she is worth no better!

DAGNY. That meanest thou not; bethink thee she is thy foster-child.

ORNULF. Woe worth the day when I took her under my roof! Jokul's words are coming true.

SIGURD. Jokul's?

ORNULF. Ay, her father's. When I gave him his death-wound he fell back upon the sward, and fixed his eyes on on me and sang: —

> Jokul's kin for Jokul's slayer
> many a woe shall still be weaving;
> Jokul's hoard whoe'er shall harry
> heartily shall rue his rashness.

When he had sung that, he was silent a while, and laughed; and thereupon he died.

SIGURD. Why should'st thou heed his words?

ORNULF. Who knows? The story goes, and many believe it, that Jokul gave his children a wolf's heart to eat, that they might be fierce and fell; and Hiordis has surely had her share, that one can well see. (Breaks off, on looking out towards the right.) Gunnar! —Are we two to meet again!

GUNNAR (enters). Ay, Ornulf, think of me what thou wilt, but I cannot part from thee as thy foe.

ORNULF. What is thy purpose?

GUNNAR. To hold out the hand of fellowship to thee ere thou depart. Hear me all of you: go with me to my homestead, and be my guests as long as ye will. We lack not meat or drink or sleeping-room, and there shall be no talk of our quarrel either to-day or to-morrow.

SIGURD. But Hiordis — —?

GUNNAR. Yields to my will; she changed her thought on the homeward way, and deemed, as I did, that we would soon be at one if ye would but be our guests.

DAGNY. Yes, yes; let it be so.

SIGURD (doubtfully). But I know not whether — —

DAGNY. Gunnar is thy foster-brother; little I know thee if thou say him nay.

GUNNAR (to SIGURD). Thou hast been my friend where'er we fared; thou wilt not stand against me now.

DAGNY. And to depart from the land, leaving Hiordis with hate in her heart—no, no, that must we not!

GUNNAR. I have done Ornulf a great wrong; until it is made good, I cannot be at peace with myself.

SIGURD (vehemently). All else will I do for thee, Gunnar, but not stay here! (Mastering himself.) I am in King AEthelstan's service, and I must be with him in England ere the winter is out.

DAGNY. But that thou canst be, nevertheless.

GUNNAR. No man can know what lot awaits him; mayhap this is our last meeting, Sigurd, and thou wilt repent that thou didst not stand by me to the end.

DAGNY. And long will it be ere thou see me glad again, if thou set sail to-day.

SIGURD (determined). Well, be it so! It shall be as ye will, although—— But no more of that; here is my hand; I will stay to feast with thee and Hiordis.

GUNNAR (shakes his hand). Thanks, Sigurd, I never doubted thee. —And thou, Ornulf, dost thou say likewise?

ORNULF (unappeased). I shall think upon it. Bitterly has Hiordis wounded me; —I will not answer to-day.

GUNNAR. It is well, old warrior; Sigurd and Dagny will know how to soothe thy brow. Now must I prepare the feast; peace be with you the while, and well met in my hall! (Goes out by the right.)

SIGURD (to himself). Hiordis has changed her thought, said he? Little he knows her; I rather deem that she is plotting—— (interrupting himself and turning to his men.) Come, follow me all to the ships; good gifts will I choose for Gunnar and his household.

DAGNY. Gifts of the best we have. And thou, father—thou shalt have no peace for me until thou yield thee. (She goes with SIGURD and his men down towards the shore at the back.)

ORNULF. Yield me? Ay, if there were no women-folk in Gunnar's house, then—— Oh, if I but knew how to pierce her armour! — Thorolf, thou here!

THOROLF (who has entered hastily). As thou seest. Is it true that thou hast met with Gunnar?

ORNULF. Yes.

THOROLF. And art at enmity with him?

ORNULF. Hm—at least with Hiordis.

THOROLF. Then be of good cheer; soon shalt thou be avenged!

ORNULF. Avenged? Who shall avenge me?

THOROLF. Listen: as I stood on board the ship, there came a man running, with a staff in his hand, and called to me: "If thou be of Ornulf's shipfolk, then greet him from Kare the Peasant, and say that now am I avenging the twain of us. " Thereupon he took a boat and rowed away, saying as he passed: "Twenty outlaws are at haven in the fiord; with them I fare southward, and ere eventide shall Hiordis be childless. "

ORNULF. He said that! Ha, now I understand; Gunnar has sent his son away; Kare is at feud with him— —

THOROLF. And now he is rowing southward to slay the boy!

ORNULF (with sudden resolution). Up all! That booty will we fight for!

THOROLF. What wilt thou do?

ORNULF. Ask me not; it shall be I, and not Kare, that will take revenge!

THOROLF. I will go with thee!

ORNULF. Nay, do thou follow with Sigurd and thy sister to Gunnar's hall.

THOROLF. Sigurd? Is he in the isle?

ORNULF. There may'st thou see his warships; we are at one—do thou go with him.

THOROLF. Among thy foes?

ORNULF. Go thou to the feast. Now shall Hiordis learn to know old Ornulf! But hark thee, Thorolf, to no one must thou speak of what I purpose; dost hear? to no one!

THOROLF. I promise.

ORNULF (takes his hand and looks at him affectionately). Farewell then, my fair boy; bear thee in courtly wise at the feast-house, that I may have honour of thee. Beware of idle babbling; but what thou sayest, let it be keen as a sword. Be friendly to those that deal with thee in friendly wise; but if thou be taunted, hold not thy peace. Drink not more than thou canst bear; but put not the horn aside when it is offered thee in measure, lest thou be deemed womanish.

THOROLF. Nay, be at ease.

ORNULF. Then away to the feast at Gunnar's hall. I too will come to the feast, and that in the guise they least think of. (Blithely to the rest.) Come, my wolf-cubs; be your fangs keen; —now shall ye have blood to drink.

(He goes off with his elder sons to the right, at the back.) (SIGURD and DAGNY come up from the ships, richly dressed for the banquet. They are followed by two men, carrying a chest, who lay it down and return as they came.)

THOROLF (looking out after his father). Now fare they all forth to fight, and I must stay behind; it is hard to be the youngest of the house. —Dagny! all hail and greetings to thee, sister mine!

DAGNY. Thorolf! All good powers! —thou art a man, grown!

THOROLF. That may I well be, forsooth, in five years——

DAGNY. Ay, true, true.

SIGURD (giving his his hand). In thee will Ornulf find a stout carl, or I mistake me.

THOROLF. Would he but prove me——!

DAGNY (smiling). He spares thee more than thou hast a mind to? Thou wast ever well-nigh too dear to him.

SIGURD. Whither has he gone?

THOROLF. Down to his ships; —he will return ere long.

SIGURD. I await my men; they are mooring my ships and bringing ashore wares.

THOROLF. There must I lend a hand!

(Goes down towards the shore.)

SIGURD (after a moment's reflection). Dagny, my wife, we are alone; I have that to tell thee which must no longer be hidden.

DAGNY (surprised). What meanest thou?

SIGURD. There may be danger in this faring to Gunnar's hall.

DAGNY. Danger? Thinkest thou that Gunnar——?

SIGURD. Nay, Gunnar is brave and true—yet better had it been that I had sailed from the isle without crossing his threshold.

DAGNY. Thou makest me fear! Sigurd, what is amiss?

SIGURD. First answer me this: the golden ring that I gave thee, where hast thou it?

DAGNY (showing it). Here, on my arm; thou badest me wear it.

SIGURD. Cast it to the bottom of the sea, so deep that none may ever set eyes on it again; else may it be the bane of many men.

DAGNY. The ring!

SIGURD (in a low voice). That evening when we carried away thy father's daughters—dost remember it?

DAGNY. Do I remember it!

SIGURD. It is of that I would speak.

DAGNY (in suspense). What is it? Say on!

SIGURD. Thou knowest there had been a feast; thou didst seek thy chamber betimes; but Hiordis still sat among the men in the feast-hall. The horn went busily round, and many a great vow was sworn. I swore to bear away a fair maid with me from Iceland; Gunnar swore the same as I, and passed the cup to Hiordis. She grasped it and stood up, and vowed this vow, that no warrior should have her to wife, save he who should go to her bower, slay the white bear that stood bound at the door, and carry her away in his arms.

DAGNY. Yes, yes; all this I know!

SIGURD. All men deemed that it might not be, for the bear was the fiercest of beasts; none but Hiordis might come near it, and it had the strength of twenty men.

DAGNY. But Gunnar slew it, and by that deed won fame throughout all lands.

SIGURD (in a low voice). He won the fame—but—*I* did the deed!

DAGNY (with a cry). Thou!

SIGURD. When the men left the feast-hall, Gunnar prayed me to come with him alone to our sleeping-place. Then said he: "Hiordis is dearer to me than all women; without her I cannot live. " I answered him: "Then go to her bower; thou knowest the vow she hath sworn. " But he said: "Life is dear to him that loves; if I should assail the bear, the end were doubtful, and I am loath to lose my life, for then should I lose Hiordis too. " Long did we talk, and the end was that Gunnar made ready his ship, while I drew my sword, donned Gunnar's harness, and went to the bower.

DAGNY (with pride and joy). And thou—thou didst slay the bear!

SIGURD. I slew him. In the bower it was dark as under a raven's wing; Hiordis deemed it was Gunnar that sat by her—she was heated with the mead—she drew a ring from her arm and gave it to me—it is that thou wearest now.

DAGNY (hesitating). And thou didst pass the night with Hiordis in her bower?

SIGURD. My sword lay drawn between us. (A short pause.) Ere the dawn, I bore Hiordis to Gunnar's ship; she dreamed not or our wiles, and he sailed away with her. Then went I to thy sleeping-place and found thee there among thy women; —what followed, thou knowest; I sailed from Iceland with a fair maid, as I had sworn, and from that day hast thou stood faithfully at my side whithersoever I might wander.

DAGNY (much moved). My brave husband! And that great deed was thine! —Oh, I should have known it; none but thou would have dared! Hiordis, that proud and stately woman, couldst thou have won, yet didst choose me! Now wouldst thou be tenfold dearer to me, wert thou not already dearer than all the world.

SIGURD. Dagny, my sweet wife, now thou knowest all—that is needful. I could not but warn thee; for that ring—Hiordis must never set eyes on it! Wouldst thou do my will, then cast it from thee—into the depths of the sea.

DAGNY. Nay, Sigurd, it is too dear to me; is it not thy gift? But be thou at ease, I shall hide it from every eye, and never shall I breathe a word of what thou hast told me.

(THOROLF comes up from the ships, with SIGURD'S men.)

THOROLF. All is ready for the feast.

DAGNY. Come then, Sigurd—my brave, my noble warrior!

SIGURD. Beware, Dagny—beware! It rests with thee now whether this meeting shall end peacefully or in bloodshed. (Cheerfully to the others.) Away then, to the feast in Gunnar's hall!

(Goes out with DAGNY to the right; the others follow.)

ACT SECOND.

(The feast-room in GUNNAR'S house. The entrance-door is in the back; smaller doors in the side-walls. In front, on the left, the greater high-seat; opposite it on the right, the lesser. In the middle of the floor, a wood fire is burning on a built-up hearth. In the background, on both sides of the door, are daises for the women of the household. From each of the high-seats, a long table, with benches, stretches backwards, parallel with the wall. It is dark outside; the fire lights the room.)

(HIORDIS and DAGNY enter from the right.)

DAGNY. Nay, Hiordis, I cannot understand thee. Thou hast shown me all the house; I know not what thing thou lackest, and all thou hast is fair and goodly; —then why bemoan thy lot?

HIORDIS. Cage an eagle and it will bite at the wires, be they of iron or of gold.

DAGNY. In one thing at least thou art richer than I; thou hast Egil, thy little son.

HIORDIS. Better no child, than one born in shame.

DAGNY. In shame?

HIORDIS. Dost thou forgot thy father's saying? Egil is the son of a leman; that was his word.

DAGNY. A word spoken in wrath—why wilt thou heed it?

HIORDIS. Nay, nay, Ornulf was right; Egil is weak; one can see he is no freeborn child.

DAGNY. Hiordis, how canst thou——?

HIORDIS (unheeding). Thus is shame sucked into the blood, like the venom of a snake-bite. Of another mettle are the freeborn sons of mighty men. I have heard of a queen that took her son and sewed his kirtle fast to his flesh, yet he never blinked an eye. (With a look of cruelty.) Dagny, that will I try with Egil!

DAGNY (horrified). Hiordis, Hiordis!

HIORDIS (laughing). Ha-ha-ha! Dost thou think I meant my words? (Changing her tone.) But, believe me or not as thou wilt, there are times when such deeds seem to lure me; it must run in the blood, — for I am of the race of the Jotuns, [1] they say. —Come, sit thou here, Dagny. Far hast thou wandered in these five long years; tell me, thou hast ofttimes been a guest in the halls of kings?

[1] The giants or Titans of Scandinavian mythology.

DAGNY. Many a time—and chiefly with AEthelstan of England.

HIORDIS. And everywhere thou hast been held in honour, and hast sat in the highest seats at the board?

DAGNY. Doubtless. As Sigurd's wife— —

HIORDIS. Ay, ay—a famous man is Sigurd—though Gunnar stands above him.

DAGNY. Gunnar?

HIORDIS. One deed did Gunnar do that Sigurd shrank from. But let that be! Tell me, when thou didst go a-viking with Sigurd, when thou didst hear the sword-blades sing in the fierce war-game, when the blood streamed red on the deck—came there not over thee an untameable longing to plunge into the strife? Didst thou not don harness and take up arms?

DAGNY. Never! How canst thou think it? I, a woman!

HIORDIS. A woman, a woman, —who knows what a woman may do! —But one thing thou canst tell me, Dagny, for that thou surely knowest: when a man clasps to his breast the woman he loves—is it true that her blood burns, that her bosom throbs—that she swoons in a shuddering ecstasy?

DAGNY (blushing). Hiordis, how canst thou— —!

HIORDIS. Come, tell me— —!

DAGNY. Surely thou thyself hast known it.

HIORDIS. Ay once, and only once; it was that night when Gunnar sat with me in my bower; he crushed me in his arms till his byrnie burst, and then, then——!

DAGNY (exclaiming). What! Sigurd——!

HIORDIS. Sigurd? What of Sigurd? I spoke of Gunnar—that night when he bore me away——

DAGNY (collecting herself). Yes, yes, I remember—I know well——

HIORDIS. That was the only time; never, never again! I deemed I was bewitched; for that Gunnar could clasp a woman—— (Stops and looks at DAGNY.) What ails thee? Methinks thou turnest pale and red!

DARNY. Nay, nay!

HIORDIS (without noticing her). The merry viking-raid should have been *my* lot; it had been better for me, and—mayhap for all of us. That were life, full and rich life! Dost thou not wonder, Dagny, to find me here alive? Art not afraid to be alone with me in the hall? Deem'st thou not that I must have died in all these years, and that it is my ghost that stands at thy side?

DAGNY (painfully affected). Come—let us go—to the others.

HIORDIS (seizing her by the arm). No, stay! Seems it not strange to thee, Dagny, that any woman can yet live after five such nights?

DAGNY. Five nights?

HIORDIS. Here in the north each night is a whole winter long. (Quickly and with an altered expression.) Yet the place is fair enough, doubt it not! Thou shalt see sights here such as thou hast not seen in the halls of the English king. We shall be together as sisters whilst thou bidest with me; we shall go down to the sea when the storm begins once more; thou shalt see the billows rushing upon the land like wild, white-maned horses—and then the whales far out in the offing! They dash one against another like steel-clad knights! Ha, what joy to be a witching-wife and ride on the whale's back—to speed before the skiff, and wake the storm, and lure men to the deeps with lovely songs of sorcery!

DAGNY. Fie, Hiordis, how canst thou talk so!

HIORDIS. Canst thou sing sorceries, Dagny?

DAGNY (with horror). I!

HIORDIS. I trow thou canst; how else didst thou lure Sigurd to thee?

DAGNY. Thou speakest shameful things; let me go!

HIORDIS (holding her back). Because I jest! Nay, hear me to the end!
Think, Dagny, what it is to sit by the window in the eventide and
hear the kelpie[1] wailing in the boat-house; to sit waiting and
listening for the dead men's ride to Valhal; for their way lies past us
here in the north. They are the brave men that fell in fight, the strong
women that did not drag out their lives tamely, like thee and me;
they sweep through the storm-night on their black horses, with
jangling bells! (Embraces DAGNY, and presses her wildly in her
arms.) Ha, Dagny! think of riding the last ride on so rare a steed!

[1] "Draugen, " a vague and horrible sea-monster.

DAGNY (struggling to escape). Hiordis, Hiordis! Let me go! I will
not hear thee!

HIORDIS (laughing). Weak art thou of heart, and easily affrighted.

(GUNNAR enters from the back, with SIGURD and THOROLF.)

GUNNAR. Now, truly, are all things to my very mind! I have found
thee again, Sigurd, my brave brother, as kind and true as of old. I
have Ornulf's son under my roof, and the old man himself follows
speedily after; is it not so?

THOROLF. So he promised.

GUNNAR. Then all I lack is that Egil should be here.

THOROLF. 'Tis plain thou lovest the boy, thou namest him so oft.

GUNNAR. Truly I love him; he is my only child; and he is like to
grow up fair and kindly.

The Vikings of Helgeland

HIORDIS. But no warrior.

GUNNAR. Nay—that thou must not say.

SIGURD. I marvel thou didst send him from thee——

GUNNAR. Would that I had not! (Half aside.) But thou knowest, Sigurd, he who loves overmuch, takes not always the manliest part. (Aloud.) I had few men in my house, and none could be sure of his life when it was known that Ornulf lay in the cove with a ship of war.

HIORDIS. One thing I know that ought first to be made safe, life afterwards.

THOROLF. And that is——?

HIORDIS. Honour and fame among men.

GUNNAR. Hiordis!

SIGURD. It shall not be said of Gunnar that he has risked his honour by doing this.

GUNNAR (sternly). None shall make strife between me and Ornulf's kinsfolk!

HIORDIS (smiling). Hm; tell me, Sigurd—can thy ship sail with any wind?

SIGURD. Ay, when it is cunningly steered.

HIORDIS. Good! I too will steer my ship cunningly, and make my way whither I will.

(Retires towards the back.)

DAGNY (whispers, uneasily). Sigurd, let us hence—this very night!

SIGURD. It is too late now; it was thou that——

DAGNY. Then I held Hiordis dear; but now——; I have heard her speak words I shudder to think of.

(SIGURD'S men, with other guests, men and women, house-carls and handmaidens, enter from the back.)

GUNNAR (after a short pause for the exchange of greetings and so forth). Now to the board! My chief guest, Ornulf of the Fiords, comes later; so Thorolf promises.

HIORDIS (to the house-folk). Pass ale and mead around, that hearts may wax merry and tongues may be loosened.

(GUNNAR leads SIGURD to the high-seat on the right. DAGNY seats herself on SIGURD'S right, HIORDIS opposite him at the other side of the same table. THOROLF is in like manner ushered to a place at the other table, and thus sits opposite GUNNAR, who occupies the greater high-seat. The others take their seats further back.)

HIORDIS (after a pause in which they drink with each other and converse quietly across the tables). It seldom chances that so many brave men are seated together, as I see to-night in our hall. It were fitting, then, that we should essay the old pastime: Let each man name his chief exploit, that all may judge which is the mightiest.

GUNNAR. That is an ill custom at a drinking-feast; it will oft breed strife.

HIORDIS. Little did I deem that Gunnar was afraid.

SIGURD. That no one deems; but it were long ere we came to an end, were we all to tell of our exploits, so many as we be. Do thou rather tell us, Gunnar, of thy journey to Biarmeland; 'tis no small exploit to fare so far to the north, and gladly would we hear of it.

HIORDIS. The journey to Biarmeland is chapman's work, and little worth to be named among warriors. Nay, do thou begin, Sigurd, if thou would'st not have me deem that thou shrinkest from hearing my husband's praise! Say on; name that one of thy deeds which thou dost prize the highest.

SIGURD. Well, since thou will have it so, so must it be. Let it be told, then, that I lay a-viking among the Orkneys; there came foemen against us, but we swept them from their ships, and I fought alone against eight men.

HIORDIS. Good was that deed; but wast thou fully armed?

SIGURD. Fully armed, with axe, spear, and sword.

HIORDIS. Still the deed was good. Now must thou, my husband, name that which thou deemest the greatest among thy exploits.

GUNNAR (unwillingly). I slew two berserkers who had seized a merchant-ship; and thereupon I sent the captive chapmen home, giving them there ship freely, without ransom. The King of England deemed well of that deed; he said that I had done hounourably, and gave me thanks and good gifts.

HIORDIS. Nay truly, Gunnar, a better deed than that couldst thou name.

GUNNAR (vehemently). I will boast of no other deed! Since last I fared from Iceland I have lived at peace and traded in merchandise. No more word on this matter!

HIORDIS. If thou thyself wilt hide thy renown, thy wife shall speak.

GUNNAR. Peace, Hiordis—I command thee!

HIORDIS. Sigurd fought with eight men, being fully armed; Gunnar came to my bower in the black night, slew the bear that had twenty men's strength, and yet had but a short sword in his hand.

GUNNAR (violently agitated). Woman, not a word more!

DAGNY (softly). Sigurd, wilt thou bear——?

SIGURD (likewise). Be still!

HIORDIS (to the company). And now, ye brave men—which is the mightier, Sigurd or Gunnar?

GUNNAR. Silence!

HIORDIS (loudly). Speak out; I have the right to crave your judgement.

AN OLD MAN (among the guests). If the truth be told, then is Gunnar's deed greater than all other deeds of men; Gunnar is the mightiest warrior, and Sigurd is second to him.

GUNNAR (with a glance across the table). Ah, Sigurd, Sigurd, didst thou but know— —!

DAGNY (softly). This is too much—even for a friend!

SIGURD. Peace, wife! (Aloud, to the others.) Ay truly, Gunnar is the most honourable of all men; so would I esteem him to my dying day, even had he never done that deed; for that I hold more lightly than ye.

HIORDIS. There speaks thy envy, Sigurd Viking!

SIGURD (smiling). Mightily art thou mistaken. (Kindly, to GUNNAR, drinking to him across the table.) Hail, noble Gunnar; our friendship shall stand fast, whosoever may seek to break it.

HIORDIS. No one, that I wot of, has such a thought.

SIGURD. Say not that; I could almost find it in me to think that thou hadst bidden us hither to stir up strife.

HIORDIS. That is like thee, Sigurd; now art thou wroth that thou may'st not be held the mightiest man at the feast-board.

SIGURD. I have ever esteemed Gunnar more highly than myself.

HIORDIS. Well, well—second to Gunnar is still a good place, and— — (with a side-glance at THOROLF) had Ornulf been here, he could have had the third seat.

THOROLF. Then would Jokul, thy father, find a low place indeed; for he fell before Ornulf.

(The following dispute is carried on, by both parties, with rising and yet repressed irritation.)

HIORDIS. That shalt thou never say! Ornulf is a skald, and men whisper that he has praised himself for greater deeds than he has done.

THOROLF. Then woe to him who whispers so loudly that it comes to my ear!

HIORDIS (with a smile of provocation). Wouldst thou avenge it?

THOROLF. Ay, so that my vengeance should be told of far and wide.

HIORDIS. Then here I pledge a cup to this, that thou may'st first have a beard on thy chin.

THOROLF. Even a beardless lad is too good to wrangle with women.

HIORDIS. But too weak to fight with men; therefore thy father let thee lie by the hearth at home in Iceland, whilst thy brothers went a-viking.

THOROLF. It had been well had he kept as good an eye on thee; for then hadst thou not left Iceland a dishonoured woman.

GUNNAR AND SIGURD. Thorolf!

DAGNY (simultaneously). Brother!

HIORDIS (softly, and quivering with rage). Ha! wait—wait!

THOROLF (gives GUNNAR his hand). Be not wroth, Gunnar; evil words came to my tongue; but thy wife egged me!

DAGNY (softly and imploringly). Foster-sister, by any love thou hast ever borne me, stir not up strife!

HIORDIS (laughing). Jests must pass at the feast-board if the merriment is to thrive.

GUNNAR (who has been talking softly to THOROLF). Thou art a brave lad! (Hands him a sword which hangs beside the high-seat.) Here, Thorolf, here is a good gift for thee. Wield it well, and let us be friends.

HIORDIS. Beware how thou givest away thy weapons, Gunnar; for men may say thou dost part with things thou canst not use!

THOROLF (who has meanwhile examined the sword). Thanks for the gift, Gunnar; it shall never be drawn in an unworthy cause.

HIORDIS. If thou wilt keep that promise, then do thou never lend the sword to thy brothers.

GUNNAR. Hiordis!

HIORDIS (continuing). Neither let it hang on thy father's wall; for there it would hang with base men's weapons.

THOROLF. True enough, Hiordis—for there thy father's axe and shield have hung this many a year.

HIORDIS (mastering herself). That Ornulf slew my father, —that deed is ever on thy tongue; but if report speak true, it was scarce so honourable a deed as thou deemest.

THOROLF. Of what report dost thou speak?

HIORDIS. I dare not name it, for it would make thee wroth.

THOROLF. Then hold thy peace—I ask no better.

(Turns from her.)

HIORDIS. Nay, why should I not tell it? Is it true, Thorolf, that for three nights thy father sat in woman's weed, doing sorceries with the witch of Smalserhorn, ere he dared face Jokul in fight.

(All rise; violent excitement among the guests.)

GUNNAR, SIGURD, AND DAGNY. Hiordis!

THOROLF (bitterly exasperated). So base a lie has no man spoken of Ornulf of the Fiords! Thou thyself hast made it, for no one less venomous than thou could dream of such a thing. The blackest crime a man can do hast thou laid at my father's door. (Throwing the sword away.) There, Gunnar, take thy gift again; I can take nought from the house wherein my father is reviled.

GUNNAR. Thorolf, hear me——!

THOROLF. Let me go! But beware both thou and Hiordis; for my father has now in his power one whom ye hold dearest of all!

HIORDIS (starting). Thy father has — —!

GUNNAR (with a cry). What sayst thou!

SIGURD (vehemently). Where is Ornulf?

THOROLF (with mocking laughter). Gone southward — with my brothers.

GUNNAR. Southward!

HIORDIS (shrieking). Gunnar! Ornulf has slain Egil, our son.

GUNNAR. Slain! — Egil slain! Then woe to Ornulf and all his race! Thorolf, speak out; — is this true?

SIGURD. Gunnar, Gunnar — hear me!

GUNNAR. Speak out, if thou care for thy life!

THOROLF. Thou canst not fright me! Wait till my father comes; he shall plant a mark of shame over against Gunnar's house! And meanwhile, Hiordis, do thou cheer thee with these words I heard to-day: "Ere eventide shall Gunnar and his wife be childless. "

(Goes out by the back.)

GUNNAR (in the deepest pain). Slain — slain! My little Egil slain!

HIORDIS (wildly). And thou — dost thou let him go? Let Egil, thy child, lie unavenged! Then wert thou the dastard of dastards — —!

GUNNAR (as if beside himself). A sword — an axe! It is the last message he shall bring!

(Seizes an axe from the bystanders and rushes out.)

SIGURD (about to follow). Gunnar, hold thy hand!

34

HIORDIS (holding him back). Stay, stay! The men will part them; I know Gunnar!

(A cry from the crowd, which has flocked together at the main door.)

SIGURD AND DAGNY. What is it?

A VOICE AMONG THE CROWD. Thorolf has fallen.

SIGURD. Thorolf! Ha, let me go!

DAGNY. My brother! Oh, my brother!

(SIGURD is on the point of rushing out. At the same moment, the crowd parts, GUNNAR enters, and throws down the axe at the door.)

GUNNAR. Now it is done. Egil is avenged!

SIGURD. Well for thee if thy hand has not been too hasty.

GUNNAR. Mayhap, mayhap; but Egil, Egil, my sweet boy!

HIORDIS. Now must we arm us, and seek help among our friends; for Thorolf has many avengers.

GUNNAR (gloomily). He will be his own worst avenger; he will haunt me night and day.

HIORDIS. Thorolf got his reward. Kinsmen must suffer for kinsmen's deeds.

GUNNAR. True, true; but this I know, my mind was lighter ere this befell.

HIORDIS. This first night[1] is ever the worst; —Ornulf has sought his revenge by shameful wiles; he would not come against us in open strife; he feigned to be peacefully-minded; and then he falls upon our defenceless child! Ha, I saw more clearly than ye; well I deemed that Ornulf was evil-minded and false; I had good cause to egg thee on against him and all his faithless tribe!

[1] Literally the "blood-night. "

GUNNAR (fiercely). That hadst thou! My vengeance is poor beside Ornulf's crime. He has lost Thorolf, but he has six sons left— and I have none—none!

A HOUSE-CARL (enters hastily from the back). Ornulf of the Fiords is at hand!

GUNNAR. Ornulf!

HIORDIS AND SEVERAL MEN. To arms! to arms!

DAGNY (simultaneously). My father!

SIGURD (as if seized by a foreboding). Ornulf——! Ah, Gunnar, Gunnar!

GUNNAR (draws his sword). Up all my men! Vengeance for Egil's death!

(ORNULF enters, with EGIL in his arms.)

GUNNAR (with a shriek). Egil!

ORNULF. Here I bring thee little Egil.

ALL (one to another). Egil! Egil alive!

GUNNAR (letting his sword fall). Woe is me! what have I done?

DAGNY. Oh, Thorolf, my brother!

SIGURD. I knew it! I knew it!

ORNULF (setting EGIL down). There, Gunnar, hast thou thy pretty boy again.

EGIL. Father! Old Ornulf would not do me ill, as thou saidst when I went away.

ORNULF (to HIORDIS). Now have I atoned for thy father; now surely there may be peace between us.

HIORDIS (with repressed emotion). Mayhap!

GUNNAR (as if waking up). Is it a ghastly dream that maddens me! Thou—thou bringest Egil home!

ORNULF. As thou seest; but in truth he has been near his death.

GUNNAR. That I know.

ORNULF. And hast no more joy in his return?

GUNNAR. Had he come sooner, I had been glad indeed. But tell me all that has befallen!

ORNULF. That is soon done. Kare the Peasant was plotting evil against you; with other caitiffs he fared southward after Egil.

GUNNAR. Kare! (To himself.) Ha, now I understand Thorolf's words!

ORNULF. His purpose came to my ears; I needs must thwart so black a deed. I would not give atonement for Jokul, and, had things so befallen, I had willingly slain thee, Gunnar, in single combat—yet I could not but protect thy child. With my sons, I hasted after Kare.

SIGURD (softly). An accursed deed has here been done.

ORNULF. When I came up with him, Egil's guards lay bound; thy son was already in thy foemen's hand, and they would not long have spared him. Hot was the fight! Seldom have I given and taken keener strokes; Kare and two men fled inland; the rest sleep safely, and will be hard to waken.

GUNNAR (in eager suspense). But thou—thou, Ornulf——?

ORNULF (gloomily). Six sons followed me into the fight.

GUNNAR (breathlessly). But homewards——?

ORNULF. None.

GUNNAR (appalled). None! (Softly.) And Thorolf, Thorolf!

(Deep emotion among the bystanders. HIORDIS shows signs of a violent mental struggle; DAGNY weeps silently by the high-seat on the right. SIGURD stands beside her, painfully agitated.)

ORNULF (after a short pause). It is hard for a many-branching pine to be stripped in a single storm. But men die and men live; —I will drink to my sons' memory. (One of SIGURD'S men hands him a horn.) Hail to you where now ye ride, my bold sons! Close upon your heels shall the copper-gates not clang, for ye come to the hall with a great following. (Drinks, and hands back the horn.) And now home to Iceland! Ornulf has fought his last fight; the old tree has but one green branch left, and it must be shielded warily. Where is Thorolf?

EGIL (to his father). Ay, show me Thorolf! Ornulf told me he would carve me a ship with many, many warriors on board.

ORNULF. I praise all good wights that Thorolf came not with us; for if he too—nay, strong though I be, that had been too heavy for me to bear. But why comes he not? He was ever the first to meet his father; for both of us it seemed we could not live without each other a single day.

GUNNAR. Ornulf, Ornulf!

ORNULF (with growing uneasiness). Ye stand all silent, I mark it now. What ails you? Where is Thorolf?

DAGNY. Sigurd, Sigurd—this will be the direst blow to him!

GUNNAR (struggling with himself). Old man! —No—— —— and yet, it cannot be hid——

ORNULF (vehemently). My son! Where is he!

GUNNAR. Thorolf is slain!

ORNULF. Slain! Thorolf? Thorolf? Ha, thou liest!

GUNNAR. I would give my warmest heart-blood to know him alive!

HIORDIS (to ORNULF). Thorolf was himself to blame for what befell; with dark sayings he gave us to wit that thou hadst fallen upon Egil and slain him; —we had parted half in wrath, and thou hast ere now brought death among my kindred. And moreover— Thorolf bore himself at the feast like a wanton boy; he brooked not our jesting, and spoke many evil things. Not till then did Gunnar wax wroth; not till then did he raise his hand upon thy son; and well I wot that he had good and lawful ground for that deed.

ORNULF (calmly). Well may we see that thou art a woman, for thou usest many words. To what end? If Thorolf is slain, then is his saga over.

EGIL. If Thorolf is slain, I shall have no warriors.

ORNULF. Nay, Egil—we have lost our warriors, but thou and I. (To HIORDIS.) Thy father sang:

> Jokul's kin for Jokul's slayer
> many a woe shall still be weaving.

Well has thou wrought that his words should come true. (Pauses a moment, then turns to one of the men.) Where got he his death-wound?

THE MAN. Right across his brow.

ORNULF (pleased). Hm; that is an honourable spot; he did not turn his back. But fell he sideways, or in towards Gunnar's feet?

THE MAN. Half sideways and half towards Gunnar.

ORNULF. That bodes but half vengeance; well well, —we shall see!

GUNNAR (approaching). Ornulf, I know well that all my goods were naught against thy loss; but crave of me what thou wilt— —

ORNULF (sternly interrupting him). Give me Thorolf's body, and let me go! Where lies he?

(GUNNAR points silently to the back.)

ORNULF (takes a step or two, but turns and says in a voice of thunder to SIGURD, DAGNY, and others who are preparing to follow him, sorrowing). Stay! Think ye Ornulf will be followed by a train of mourners, like a whimpering woman? Stay, I say! —I can bear my Thorolf alone. (With calm strength.) Sonless I go; but none shall say that he saw me bowed. (He goes slowly out.)

HIORDIS (with forced laughter). Ay, let him go as he will; we shall scarce need many men to face him should he come with strife again! Now, Dagny—I wot it is the last time thy father shall sail from Iceland on such a quest!

SIGURD (indignant). Oh, shame!

DAGNY (likewise). And thou canst scoff at him—scoff at him, after all that has befallen?

HIORDIS. A deed once done, 'tis wise to praise it. This morning I swore hate and vengeance against Ornulf; —the slaying of Jokul I might have forgotten—all, save that he cast shame upon my lot. He called me a leman; if it *be* so, it shames me not; for Gunnar is mightier now than thy father; he is greater and more famous than Sigurd, thine own husband!

DAGNY (in wild indignation). There thou errest, Hiordis—and even now shall all men know that thou dwellest under a weakling's roof!

SIGURD (vehemently). Dagny, beware!

GUNNAR. A weakling!

DAGNY. It shall no longer be hidden; I held my peace till thou didst scoff at my father and my dead brothers; I held my peace while Ornulf was here, lest he should learn that Thorolf fell by a dastard's hand. But now—praise Gunnar nevermore for that deed in Iceland; for Gunnar is a weakling! The sword that lay drawn between thee and the bear-slayer hangs at my husband's side—and the ring thou didst take from thy arm thou gavest to Sigurd. (Takes it off and holds if aloft.) Behold it!

HIORDIS (wildly). Sigurd!

THE CROWD. Sigurd! Sigurd did the deed!

HIORDIS (quivering with agitation). He! he! —Gunnar, is this true?

GUNNAR (with lofty calm). It is all true save only that I am a weakling; I am neither a weakling nor a coward.

SIGURD (moved). That art thou not, Gunnar! That hast thou never been! (To the rest.) Away, my men! Away from here!

DAGNY (at the door, to HIORDIS). Who is now the mightiest man at the board—my husband or thine?

HIORDIS (to herself). Now have I but one thing left to do—but one deed to brood upon: Sigurd or I must die!

ACT THIRD.

(The hall in GUNNAR'S house. It is day.) (HIORDIS sits on the bench in front of the smaller high-seat busy weaving a bow-string; on the table lie a bow and some arrows.)

HIORDIS (pulling at the bow-string). It is tough and strong; (with a glance at the arrows) the shaft is both keen and well-weighted — (lets her hands fall in her lap) but where is the hand that — —! (Vehemently.) Befooled, befooled by him — by Sigurd! I must hate him more than others, that can I well mark; but ere many days have passed I will — — (Meditating.) Ay, but the arm, the arm that shall do the deed — —?

(GUNNAR enters, silent and thoughtful, from the back.)

HIORDIS (after a short pause). How goes it with thee, my husband?

GUNNAR. Ill, Hiordis; I cannot away with that deed of yesterday; it lies heavy on my heart.

HIORDIS. Do as I do; get thee some work to busy thee.

GUNNAR. Doubtless I must.

(A pause; GUNNAR paces up and down the hall, notices what HIORDIS is doing, and approaches her.)

GUNNAR. What dost thou there?

HIORDIS (without looking up). I am weaving a bow-string; canst thou not see?

GUNNAR. A bow-string — of thine own hair?

HIORDIS (smiling). Great deeds are born with every hour in these times; yesterday thou didst slay my foster-brother, and I have woven this since day-break.

GUNNAR. Hiordis, Hiordis!

HIORDIS (looking up). What is amiss?

42

GUNNAR. Where wast thou last night?

HIORDIS. Last night?

GUNNAR. Thou wast not in the sleeping-room.

HIORDIS. Know'st thou that?

GUNNAR. I could not sleep; I tossed in restless dreams of that— that which befell Thorolf. I dreamt that he came— — No matter; I awakened. Then meseemed I heard a strange, fair song through all the house; I arose; I stole hither to the door; here I saw thee sitting by the log-fire—it burned blue and red—fixing arrow-heads, and singing sorceries over them.

HIORDIS. The work was not wasted; for strong is the breast that must be pierced this day.

GUNNAR. I understand thee well; thou wouldst have Sigurd slain.

HIORDIS. Hm, mayhap.

GUNNAR. Thou shalt never have thy will. I shall keep peace with Sigurd, howe'er thou goad me.

HIORDIS (smiling). Dost think so?

SIGURD. I know it!

HIORDIS (hands him the bow-string). Tell me, Gunnar—canst loose this knot?

GUNNAR (tries it). Nay it is too cunningly and firmly woven.

HIORDIS (rising). The Norns[1] weave yet more cunningly; their web is still harder to unravel.

[1] The "Nornir" were the Fates of northern mythology.

GUNNAR. Dark are the ways of the Mighty Ones; —neither thou nor I know aught of them.

HIORDIS. Yet one thing I know surely: that to both of us must Sigurd's life be baleful.

(A pause; GUNNAR stands lost in thought.)

HIORDIS (who has been silently watching him). Of what thinkest thou?

GUNNAR. Of a dream I had of late. Methought I had done the deed thou cravest; Sigurd lay slain on the earth; thou didst stand beside him, and thy face was wondrous pale. Then said I: "Art thou glad, now that I have done thy will? " But thou didst laugh and answer: "Blither were I didst thou, Gunnar, lie there in Sigurd's stead. "

HIORDIS (with forced laughter). Ill must thou know me if such a senseless dream can make thee hold thy hand.

GUNNAR. Hm! —Tell me, Hiordis, what thinkest thou of this hall?

HIORDIS. To speak truly, Gunnar, —it sometimes seems to me to be straitened.

GUNNAR. Ay, ay, so I have thought; we are one too many.

HIORDIS. Two, mayhap.

GUNNAR (who has not heard her last words). But that shall be remedied.

HIORDIS (looks at him interrogatively). Remedied? Then thou art minded to— —?

GUNNAR. To fit out my warships and put to sea; I will win back the honour I have lost because thou wast dearer to me than all beside.

HIORDIS (thoughtfully). Thou wilt put to sea? Ay, so it may be best for us both.

GUNNAR. Even from the day we sailed from Iceland, I saw that it would go ill with us. Thy soul is strong and proud; there are times when I well nigh fear thee; yet, it is strange—chiefly for that do I hold thee so dear. Dread enwraps thee like a spell; methinks thou could'st lure me to the blackest deeds, and all would seem good to me that thou didst crave. (Shaking his head reflectively.) Unfathomable is the Norn's rede; Sigurd should have been thy husband.

HIORDIS (vehemently). Sigurd!

GUNNAR. Yes, Sigurd. Vengefulness and hatred blind thee, else would'st thou prize him better. Had I been like Sigurd, I could have made life bright for thee.

HIORDIS (with strong but suppressed emotion). That—that deemest thou Sigurd could have done?

GUNNAR. He is strong of soul, and proud as thou to boot.

HIORDIS (violently). If that be so—(Collecting herself.) No matter, no matter! (With a wild outburst.) Gunnar, take Sigurd's life!

GUNNAR. Never!

HIORDIS. By fraud and falsehood thou mad'st me thy wife—that shall be forgotten! Five joyless years have I spent in this house— all shall be forgotten from the day when Sigurd lives no more!

GUNNAR. From my hand he need fear no harm. (Shrinks back involuntarily.) Hiordis, Hiordis, tempt me not!

HIORDIS. Then must I find another avenger; Sigurd shall not live long to flout at me and thee! (Clenching her hands in convulsive rage.) With her—that simpleton—with her mayhap he is even now sitting alone, dallying, and laughing at us; speaking of the bitter wrong that was done me when in thy stead he bore me away; telling how he laughed over his guile as he stood in my dark bower, and I knew him not!

GUNNAR. Nay, nay, he does not so!

HIORDIS (firmly). Sigurd and Dagny must die! I cannot breathe till they are gone! (Comes close up to him, with sparkling eyes, and speaks passionately, but in a whisper.) Would'st thou help me with *that*, Gunnar, then should I live in love with thee; then should I clasp thee in such warm and wild embraces as thou hast never dreamt of!

GUNNAR (wavering). Hiordis! Would'st thou — —

HIORDIS. Do the deed, Gunnar—and the heavy days shall be past. I will no longer quit the hall when thou comest, no longer speak harsh things and quench thy smile when thou art glad. I will clothe me in furs and costly silken robes. When thou goest to war, I will ride by thy side. At the feast I will sit by thee and fill thy horn, and drink to thee and sing fair songs to make glad thy heart!

GUNNAR (almost overcome). Is it true? Thou wouldst— —!

HIORDIS. More than that, trust me, ten times more! Give me revenge! Revenge on Sigurd and Dagny, and I will— — (Stops as she sees the door open.) Dagny—comest thou here!

DAGNY (from the back). Haste thee, Gunnar! Call thy men to arms!

GUNNAR. To arms! Against whom?

DAGNY. Kare the Peasant is coming, and many outlaws with him; he means thee no good; Sigurd has barred his way for the time; but who can tell— —

GUNNAR (moved). Sigurd has done this for me!

DAGNY. Sigurd is ever thy faithful friend.

GUNNAR. And we, Hiordis—we, who thought to— —! It is as I say— there is a spell in all thy speech; no deed but seemeth fair to me, when thou dost name it.

DAGNY (astonished). What meanest thou?

GUNNAR. Nothing, nothing! Thanks for thy tidings, Dagny; I go to gather my men together. (Turns towards the door, but stops and comes forward again.) Tell me—how goes it with Ornulf?

DAGNY (bowing her head). Ask me not. Yesterday he bore Thorolf's body to the ships; now he is raising a grave-mound on the shore; — there shall his son be laid.

(GUNNAR says nothing and goes out by the back.)

DAGNY. Until evening there is no danger. (Coming nearer.) Hiordis, I have another errand in thy house; it is to thee I come.

HIORDIS. To me? After all that befell yesterday?

DAGNY. Just because of that. Hiordis, foster-sister, do not hate me; forget the words that sorrow and evil spirits placed in my mouth; forgive me all the wrong I have done thee; for, trust me, I am tenfold more hapless than thou!

HIORDIS. Hapless—thou! Sigurd's wife!

DAGNY. It was *my* doing, all that befell—the stirring up of strife, and Thorolf's death, and all the scorn that fell upon Gunnar and thee. Mine is all the guilt! Woe upon me! —I have lived so happily; but after this day I shall never know joy again.

HIORDIS (as if seized by a sudden thought). But before—in these five long years—all that time hast thou been happy?

DAGNY. Canst thou doubt it?

HIORDIS. Hm; yesterday I doubted it not; but— —

DAGNY. What meanest thou?

HIORDIS. Nay, 'tis nought; let us speak of other matters.

DAGNY. No truly. Hiordis, tell me— —!

HIORDIS. It will profit thee little; but since thou wilt have it so— — (With a malignant expression.) Canst thou remember once, over in Iceland—we had followed with Ornulf thy father to the Council, and we sat with our playmates in the Council Hall, as is the manner of women. Then came two strangers into the hall.

DAGNY. Sigurd and Gunnar.

HIORDIS. They greeted us in courteous fashion, and sat on the bench beside us; and there passed between us much merry talk. There were some who must needs know why these two vikings came thither, and if they were not minded to take them wives there in the island. Then said Sigurd: "It will be hard for me to find the woman that shall be to my mind. " Ornulf laughed, and said there was no lack of high-born and well-dowered women in Iceland; but Sigurd answered: "The warrior needs a high-souled wife. She whom I choose must not rest content with a humble lot; no honour must seem to high for her to strive for; she must go with me gladly a-viking; war-weed must she wear; she must egg me on to strife, and never wink her eyes where sword-blades lighten; for if she be faint-hearted, scant honour will befall me. " Is it not true, so Sigurd spake?

DAGNY (hesitatingly). True, he did—but——

HIORDIS. *Such* was she to be, the woman who could make life fair to him; and then—(with a scornful smile) then he chose thee!

DAGNY (starting, as in pain). Ha, thou wouldst say that——?

HIORDIS. Doubtless thou has proved thyself proud and high-souled; hast claimed honour of all, that Sigurd might be honoured in thee— is it not so?

DAGNY. Nay, Hiordis, but——

HIORDIS. Thou hast egged him on to great deeds, followed him in war- weed, and joyed to be where the strife raged hottest—hast thou not?

DAGNY (deeply moved). No, no!

HIORDIS. Hast thou, then, been faint of heart, so that Sigurd has been put to shame?

DAGNY (overpowered). Hiordis, Hiordis!

HIORDIS (smiling scornfully). Yet thy lot has been a happy one all these years; —think'st thou that Sigurd can say the same?

DAGNY. Torture me not. Woe is me! thou hast made me see myself too clearly.

HIORDIS. A jesting word, and at once thou art in tears! Think no more of it. Look what I have done to-day. (Takes some arrows from the table.) Are they not keen and biting—feel! I know well how to sharpen arrows, do I not?

DAGNY. And to use them too; thou strikest surely, Hiordis! All that thou hast said to me—I have never thought of before. (More vehemently.) But that Sigurd——! That for all these years I should have made his life heavy and unhonoured; —no, no, it cannot be true!

HIORDIS. Nay now, comfort thee, Dagny; indeed it is not true. Were Sigurd of the same mind as in former days, it might be true enough; for then was his whole soul bent on being the foremost man in the land; —now he is content with a lowlier lot.

DAGNY. No, Hiordis; Sigurd is high-minded now as ever; I see it well, I am not the right mate for him. He has hidden it from me; but it shall be so no longer.

HIORDIS. What wilt thou do?

DAGNY. I will no longer hang like a clog upon his feet; I will be a hindrance to him no longer.

HIORDIS. Then thou wilt——?

DAGNY. Peace; some one comes!

(A House-carl enters from the back.)

THE CARL. Sigurd Viking is coming to the hall.

HIORDIS. Sigurd! Then call Gunnar hither.

THE CARL. Gunnar has ridden forth to gather his neighbours together; for Kare the Peasant would——

HIORDIS. Good, good, I know it; go! (The Carl goes. To DAGNY, who is also going.) Whither wilt thou?

DAGNY. I will not meet Sigurd. Too well I feel that we must part; but to meet him now—no, no, I cannot!

(Goes out to the left.)

HIORDIS (looks after her in silence for a moment). And it was she I would have—— (completes her thought by a glance at the bow-string). That would have been a poor revenge; —nay, I have cut deeper now! Hm; it is hard to die, but sometimes it is harder still to live!

(SIGURD enters from the back.)

HIORDIS. Doubtless thou seekest Gunnar; be seated, he will be here even now.

(Is going.)

SIGURD. Nay, stay; it is thee I seek, rather than him.

HIORDIS. Me?

SIGURD. And 'tis well I find thee alone.

HIORDIS. If thou comest to mock me, it would sure be no hindrance to thee though the hall were full of men and women.

SIGURD. Ay, ay, well I know what thoughts thou hast of me.

HIORDIS (bitterly). I do thee wrong mayhap! Nay, nay, Sigurd, thou hast been as a poison to all my days. Bethink thee who it was that wrought that shameful guile; who it was that lay by my side in the bower, feigning love with the laugh of cunning in his heart; who it was that flung me forth to Gunnar, since for him I was good enough, forsooth—and then sailed away with the woman he held dear!

SIGURD. Man's will can do this and that; but fate rules in the deeds that shape our lives—so has it gone with us twain.

HIORDIS. True enough; evil Norns hold sway over the world; but their might is little if they find not helpers in our own heart. Happy is he who has strength to battle with the Norn—and it is that I have now in hand.

SIGURD. What mean'st thou?

HIORDIS. I will essay a trial of strength against those—those who are over me. But let us not talk more of this; I have much to do to-day. (She seats herself at the table.)

SIGURD (after a pause). Thou makest good weapons for Gunnar.

HIORDIS (with a quiet smile). Not for Gunnar, but against thee.

SIGURD. Most like it is the same thing.

HIORDIS. Ay, most like it is; for if I be a match for the Norn, then sooner or later shalt thou and Gunnar—— (breaks off, leans backwards against the table, and says with an altered ring in her voice:) Hm; knowest thou what I sometimes dream? I have often made it my pastime to limn pleasant pictures in my mind; I sit and close my eyes and think: Now comes Sigurd the Strong to the isle; — he will burn us in our house, me and my husband. All Gunnar's men have fallen; only he and I are left; they set light to the roof from without: —"A bow-shot, " cries Gunnar, "one bow-shot may save us; " — then the bow-string breaks—"Hiordis, cut a tress of thy hair and make a bow-string of it, —our life is at stake. " But then I laugh— "Let it burn, let it burn—to me, life is not worth a handful of hair! "

SIGURD. There is a strange might in all thy speech. (Approaches her.)

HIORDIS (looks coldly at him). Wouldst sit beside me?

SIGURD. Thou deemest my heart is bitter towards thee. Hiordis, this is the last time we shall have speech together; there is something that gnaws me like a sore sickness, and thus I cannot part from thee; thou must know me better.

HIORDIS. What wouldst thou?

SIGURD. Tell thee a saga.

HIORDIS. Is it sad?

SIGURD. Sad, as life itself.

HIORDIS (bitterly). What knowest thou of the sadness of life?

SIGURD. Judge when my saga is over.

HIORDIS. Then tell it me; I shall work the while.

(He sits on a low stool to her right.)

SIGURD. Once upon a time there were two young vikings, who set forth from Norway to win wealth and honour; they had sworn each other friendship; and held truly together, how far soever thy might fare.

HIORDIS. And the two young vikings hight Sigurd and Gunnar?

SIGURD. Ay, we may call them so. At last they came to Iceland; and there dwelt an old chieftain, who had come forth from Norway in King Harald's days. He had two fair women in his house; but one, his foster-daughter, was the noblest, for she was wise and strong of soul; and the vikings spoke of her between themselves, and never had they seen a fairer woman, so deemed they both.

HIORDIS (in suspense). Both? Wilt thou mock me?

SIGURD. Gunnar thought of her night and day, and that did Sigurd no less; but both held their peace, and no man could say from her bearing whether Gunnar found favour in her eyes; but that Sigurd misliked her, that was easy to discern.

HIORDIS (breathlessly). Go on, go on——!

SIGURD. Yet ever the more must Sigurd dream of her; but of that wist no man. Now it befell one evening that there was a drinking-feast; and then swore that proud woman that no man should possess her save he who wrought a mighty deed, which she named. High beat Sigurd's heart for joy; for he felt within him the strength to do that deed; but Gunnar took him apart and told him of his love; — Sigurd said naught of his, but went to the——

HIORDIS (vehemently). Sigurd, Sigurd! (Controlling herself.) And this saga—is it true?

SIGURD. True it is. One of us had to yield; Gunnar was my friend; I could do aught else. So thou becamest Gunnar's wife, and I wedded another woman.

HIORDIS. And came to love her!

SIGURD. I learned to prize her; but one woman only has Sigurd loved, and that is she who frowned upon him from the first day they met. Here ends my saga; and now let us part. —Farewell, Gunnar's wife; never shall we meet again.

HIORDIS (springing up). Stay, stay! Woe to us both; Sigurd, what hast thou done?

SIGURD (starting). I, done? What ails thee?

HIORDIS. And all this dost thou tell me now! But no—it cannot be true!

SIGURD. These are my last words to thee, and every word is true. I would not thou shouldst think hardly of me, therefore I needs must speak.

HIORDIS (involuntarily clasps her hands together and gazes at him in voiceless astonishment). Loved—loved me—thou! (Vehemently, coming close up to him.) I will not believe thee! (Looks hard at him.) Yes, it is true, and—baleful for us both!

(Hides her face in her hands, and turns away from him.)

SIGURD (terror-stricken). Hiordis!

HIORDIS (softly, struggling with tears and laughter). Nay, heed me not! This was all I meant, that— — (Lays her hand on his arm.) Sigurd, thou hast not told thy saga to the end; that proud woman thou didst tell of—she returned thy love!

SIGURD (starts backwards). Thou?

HIORDIS (with composure). Yes, Sigurd, I have loved thee, at last I understand it. Thou sayest I was ungentle and short of speech towards thee; what wouldst thou have a woman do? I could not offer thee my love, for then had I been little worthy of thee. I deemed thee ever the noblest man of men; and then to know thee another's husband—'twas that caused me the bitter pain, that myself I could not understand!

SIGURD (much moved). A baleful web has the Norn woven around us twain.

HIORDIS. The blame is thine own; bravely and firmly it becomes a man to act. When I set that hard proof for him who should win me, my thought was of thee; —yet could'st thou——!

SIGURD. I knew Gunnar's soul-sickness; I alone could heal it; —was there aught for me to choose? And yet, had I known what I now know, I scarce dare answer for myself; for great is the might of love.

HIORDIS (with animation). But now, Sigurd! —A baleful hap has held us apart all these years; now the knot is loosed; the days to come shall make good the past to us.

SIGURD (shaking his head). It cannot be; we must part again.

HIORDIS. Nay, we must not. I love thee, that may I now say unashamed; for my love is no mere dalliance, like a weak woman's; were I a man— by all the Mighty Ones, I could still love thee, even as now I do! Up then, Sigurd! Happiness is worth a daring deed; we are both free if we but will it, and then the game is won.

SIGURD. Free? What meanest thou?

HIORDIS. What is Dagny to thee? What can she be to thee? No more than I count Gunnar in my secret heart. What matters it though two worthless lives be wrecked?

SIGURD. Hiordis, Hiordis!

HIORDIS. Let Gunnar stay where he is; let Dagny fare with her father to Iceland; I will follow thee in harness of steel, withersoever thou wendest. (SIGURD makes a movement.) Not as thy wife will I follow thee; for I have belonged to another, and the woman lives that has lain by thy side. No, Sigurd, not as they wife, but like those mighty women, like Hilde's sisters, [1] will I follow thee, and fire thee to strife and to manly deeds, so that thy name shall be heard over every land. In the sword-game will I stand by thy side; I will fare forth among thy warriors on the stormy viking-raids; and when the death- song is sung, it shall tell of Sigurd and Hiordis in one!

[1] The Valkyries.

SIGURD. Once was that my fairest dream; now, it is too late. Gunnar and Dagny stand between us, and that by right. I crushed my love for Gunnar's sake; —how great soever my suffering, I cannot undo my deed. And Dagny—full of faith and trust she left her home and kindred; never must she dream that I longed for Hiordis as often as she took me to her breast.

HIORDIS. And for such a cause wilt thou lay a burden on thy life! To what end hast thou strength and might, and therewith all noble gifts of the mind? And deemest thou it can now beseem me to dwell beneath Gunnar's roof? Nay, Sigurd, trust me, there are many tasks awaiting such a man as thou. Erik is king of Norway—do thou rise against him! Many goodly warriors will join thee and swear thee fealty; with unconquerable might will we press onward, and fight and toil unresting until thou art seated on the throne of Harfager!

SIGURD. Hiordis, Hiordis, so have I dreamt in my wild youth; let it be forgotten—tempt me not!

HIORDIS (impressively). It is the Norn's will that we two shall hold together; it cannot be altered. Plainly now I see my task in life: to make thee famous over all the world. Thou hast stood before me every day, every hour of my life; I sought to tear thee out of my mind, but I lacked the might; now it is needless, now that I know thou lovest me.

SIGURD (with forced coldness). If that be so—then know—I *have* loved thee; it is past now; —I have forgot those days.

HIORDIS. Sigurd, in that thou liest! So much at least am I worth, that if thou hast loved me once, thou canst never forget it.

SIGURD (vehemently). I must; and now I will.

HIORDIS. So be it; but thou *canst* not. Thou wilt seek to hinder me, but in vain; ere evening falls, Gunnar and Dagny shall know all.

SIGURD. Ha, that wilt thou never do!

HIORDIS. That will I do!

SIGURD. Then must I know thee ill; high-souled have I ever deemed thee.

HIORDIS. Evil days breed evil thoughts; too great has been thy trust in me. I will, I must, go forth by thy side—forth to face life and strife; Gunnar's roof-tree is too low for me.

SIGURD (with emphasis). But honour between man and man hast thou highly prized. There lack not grounds for strife between me and Gunnar; say, now, that he fell by my hand, wouldst thou still make all known and follow me?

HIORDIS (starting). Wherefore askest thou?

SIGURD. Answer me first: what wouldst thou do, were I to thy husband his bane.

HIORDIS (looks hard at him). Then must I keep silence and never rest until I had seen thee slain.

SIGURD (with a smile). It is well, Hiordis—I knew it.

HIORDIS (hastily). But it can never come to pass!

SIGURD. It must come to pass; thou thyself hast cast the die for Gunnar's life and mine.

(GUNNAR, with some House-carls, enters from the back.)

GUNNAR (gloomily, to HIORDIS). See now; the seed thou hast sown is shooting bravely!

SIGURD (approaching). What is amiss with thee?

GUNNAR. Sigurd, is it thou? What is amiss? Nought but what I might well have foreseen. As soon as Dagny, thy wife, had brought tidings of Kare the Peasant, I took horse and rode to my neighbours to crave help against him.

HIORDIS (eagerly). Well?

GUNNAR. I was answered awry where'er I came: my dealings with Kare had been little to my honour, it was said; —hm, other things were said to boot, that I will not utter. —I am spurned at by all; I am thought to have done a dastard deed; men hold it a shame to make common cause with me.

SIGURD. It shall not long be held a shame; ere evening comes, thou shalt have men enough to face Kare.

GUNNAR. Sigurd!

HIORDIS (in a low voice, triumphantly). Ha, I knew it well!

SIGURD (with forced resolution). But then is there an end to the peace between us; for hearken to my words, Gunnar—thou hast slain Thorolf, my wife's kinsman, and therefore do I challenge thee to single combat[1] to-morrow at break of day.

[1] *Holmgang*—see note, p. 138 [*Holmgang*=duel.]

(HIORDIS, in violent inward emotion, makes a stride towards SIGURD, but collects herself and remains standing motionless during the following.)

GUNNAR (in extreme astonishment). To single combat——! Me! — Thou art jesting, Sigurd!

SIGURD. Thou art lawfully challenged to single combat; 'twill be a game for life or death; one of us must fall!

GUNNAR (bitterly). Ha, I understand it well. When I came, thou didst talk with Hiordis alone; she has goaded thee afresh!

SIGURD. May hap. (Half towards HIORDIS.) A high-souled woman must ever guard her husband's honour. (To the men in the background.) And do ye, house-carls, now go to Gunnar's neighbours, and say to them that to-morrow he is to ply sword-strokes with me; none dare call that man a dastard who bears arms against Sigurd Viking!

(The House-carls go out by the back.)

GUNNAR (goes quickly up to SIGURD and presses his hands, in strong emotion). Sigurd, my brave brother, now I understand thee! Thou venturest thy life for my honour, as of old for my happiness!

SIGURD. Thank thy wife; she has the largest part in what I do. To-morrow at break of day——

GUNNAR. I will meet thee. (Tenderly.) Foster-brother, wilt thou have a good blade of me? It is a gift of price.

SIGURD. I thank thee; but let it hang. —Who knows if next evening I may have any use for it.

GUNNAR (shakes his hand). Farewell, Sigurd!

SIGURD. Again farewell, and fortune befriend thee this night!

(They part. GUNNAR goes out to the right. SIGURD casts a glance at HIORDIS, and goes out by the back.)

HIORDIS (after a pause, softly and thoughtfully). To-morrow they fight! Which will fall? (After a moment's silence, she bursts forth as if seized by a strong resolution.) Let fall who will—Sigurd and I shall still be together!

ACT FOURTH.

(By the coast. It is evening; the moon breaks forth now and again, from among dark and ragged storm-clouds. At the back, a black grave-mound, newly heaped up.) (ORNULF sits on a stone, in front on the right, his head bare, his elbows resting on his knees, and his face buried in his hands. His men are digging at the mound; some give light with pine-knot torches. After a short pause, SIGURD and DAGNY enter from the boat-house, where a wood fire is burning.)

DAGNY (in a low voice). There sits he still. (Holding SIGURD back.) Nay, speak not to him!

SIGURD. Thou say'st well; it is too soon; best leave him!

DAGNY (goes over to the right, and gazes at her father in quiet sorrow). So strong was he yesterday when he bore Thorolf's body on his back; strong was he as he helped to heap the grave-mound; but when they were all laid to rest, and earth and stones piled over them—then the sorrow seized him; then seemed it of a sudden as though his fire were quenched. (Dries her tears.) Tell me, Sigurd, when thinkest thou to fare homeward to Iceland?

SIGURD. So soon as the storm abates, and my quarrel with Gunnar is ended.

DAGNY. And then wilt thou buy land and build thee a homestead, and go a-viking no more?

SIGURD. Yes, yes, —that have I promised.

DAGNY. And I may believe without doubt that Hiordis spoke falsely when she said that I was unworthy to be thy wife?

SIGURD. Yes yes, Dagny, trust thou to my word.

DAGNY. Then am I glad again, and will try to forget all the evil that here has been wrought. In the long winter evenings we will talk together of Gunnar and Hiordis, and——

SIGURD. Nay, Dagny, wouldst thou have things go well with us, do thou never speak Hiordis' name when we sit together in Iceland.

DAGNY (mildly upbraiding him). Unjust is thy hatred towards her. Sigurd, Sigurd, it is unlike thee.

ONE OF THE MEN (approaching). There now, the mound is finished.

ORNULF (as if awaking). The mound? Is it—ay, ay — —

SIGURD. Now speak to him, Dagny.

DAGNY (approaching). Father, it is cold out here; a storm is gathering to-night.

ORNULF. Hm; heed it not; the mound is close-heaped and crannyless; they lie warm in there.

DAGNY. Ay, but thou — —

ORNULF. I? I am not cold.

DAGNY. Nought hast thou eaten today; wilt thou not go in? The supper-board stands ready.

ORNULF. Let the supper-board stand; I have no hunger.

DAGNY. But to sit here so still—trust me, thou wilt take hurt of it; thou art ever wont to be stirring.

ORNULF. True, true; there is somewhat that crushes my breast; I cannot draw breath.

(He hides his face in his hands. A pause. DAGNY seats herself beside him.)

DAGNY. To-morrow wilt thou make ready thy ship and set forth for Iceland?

ORNULF (without looking up). What should I do there? Nay, I will to my sons.

DAGNY (with pain). Father!

ORNULF (raises his head). Go in and let me sit here; when the storm has played with me for a night or two, the game will be over, I ween.

SIGURD. Thou canst not think to deal thus with thyself.

ORNULF. Dost marvel that I fain would rest? My day's work is done; I have laid my sons in their grave. (Vehemently.) Go from me! —Go, go!

(He hides his face.)

SIGURD (softly, to DAGNY, who rises). Let him sit yet a while.

DAGNY. Nay, I have one rede yet untried; —I know him. (To Ornulf.) Thy day's work done, say'st thou? Nay, that it is not. Thou hast laid thy sons in the grave; —but art thou not a skald? It is meet that thou should'st sing their memory.

ORNULF (shaking his head). Sing? Nay, nay; yesterday I could sing; I am too old to-day.

DAGNY. But needs must thou; honourable men were thy sons, one and all; a song must be made of them, and that can none of our kin but thou.

ORNULF (looks inquiringly at SIGURD). To sing? What thinkest *thou*, Sigurd?

SIGURD. Meseems it is but meet; thou must e'en do as she says.

DAGNY. Thy neighbours in Iceland will deem it ill done when the grave-ale is drunk over Ornulf's children, and there is no song to sing with it. Thou hast ever time enough to follow thy sons.

ORNULF. Well well, I will try it; and thou, Dagny, give heed, that afterwards thou may'st carve the song on staves.

(The men approach with the torches, forming a group around him; he is silent for a time, reflecting; then he says:)

> Bragi's[1] gift is bitter
> when the heart is broken;
> sorrow-laden singer,

61

singing, suffers sorely.

Natheless, since the Skald-god
gave me skill in song-craft,
in a lay loud-ringing
be my loss lamented!

(Rises.)

Ruthless Norn[2] and wrathful
wrecked my life and ravaged,
wiled away my welfare,
wasted Ornulf's treasure.

Sons had Ornulf seven,
by the great gods granted;—
lonely now and life-sick
goes the greybeard, sonless.

Seven sons so stately,
bred among the sword-blades,
made a mighty bulwark
round the snow-locked sea-king.

Levelled lies the bulwark,
dead my swordsmen seven;
gone the greybeard's gladness,
desolate his dwelling.

Thorolf,—thou my last-born!
Of the bold the boldest!
Soon were spent my sorrow
so but thou wert left me!

Fair thou wast as springtide,
fond towards thy father,
waxing straight and stalwart
to so wight a warrior.

Dark and drear his death-wound
leaves my life's lone evening;
grief hath gripped my bosom
as 'twixt hurtling targes.

Nought the Norn denied me
of her rueful riches,
showering woes unstinted
over Ornulf's world-way.

Weak are now my weapons.
But, were god-might given me,
then, oh Norn, I swear it,
scarce should'st thou go scatheless!

Dire were then my vengeance;
then had dawned thy doomsday,
Norn, that now hast left me
nought but yonder grave-mound.

Nought, I said? Nay, truly,
somewhat still is Ornulf's,
since of Suttung's[3] mead-horn
he betimes drank deeply.

(With rising enthusiasm.)

Though she stripped me sonless,
one great gift she gave me—
songcraft's mighty secret,
skill to sing my sorrows.

On my lips she laid it,
goodly gift of songcraft;
loud, then, let my lay sound,
e'en where they are lying!

Hail, my stout sons seven!
Hail, as homeward ride ye!
Songcraft's glorious god-gift
stauncheth woe and wailing.

[1] Bragi, the god of poetry and eloquence.

[2] See note, [The "Norns" were the Fates of northern mythology.]

[3] Suttung was a giant who kept guard over the magic mead of poetical inspiration.

(He draws a deep breath, throws back the hair from his brow, and says calmly:)

So—so; now is Ornulf sound and strong again. (To the men.) Follow me to the supper-board, lads; we have had a heavy day's work!

(Goes with the men into the boat-house.)

DAGNY. Praised be the Mighty Ones on high that gave me so good a rede. (To SIGURD.) Wilt thou not go in?

SIGURD. Nay, I list not to. Tell me, are all things ready for to-morrow?

DAGNY. They are; a silk-sewn shroud lies on the bench; but I know full surely that thou wilt hold thee against Gunnar, so I have not wept over it.

SIGURD. Grant all good powers, that thou may'st never weep for my sake. (He stops and looks out.)

DAGNY. What art thou listening to?

SIGURD. Hear'st thou nought—*there?*

(Points towards the left.)

DAGNY. Ay, there goes a fearsome storm over the sea!

SIGURD (going up a little towards the background). Hm, there will fall hard hailstones in that storm. (Shouts.) Who comes?

KARE THE PEASANT (without on the left). Folk thou wot'st of, Sigurd Viking!

(KARE THE PEASANT, with a band of armed men, enters from the left.)

SIGURD. Whither would ye?

KARE. To Gunnar's hall.

SIGURD. As foemen?

KARE. Ay, trust me for that! Thou didst hinder me before; but now I ween thou wilt scarce do the like.

SIGURD. Maybe not.

KARE. I have heard of thy challenge to Gunnar; but if things go to my mind, weak will be his weapons when the time comes for your meeting.

SIGURD. 'Tis venturesome work thou goest about; take heed for thyself, Peasant!

KARE (with defiant laughter). Leave that to me; if thou wilt tackle thy ship to-night, we will give thee light for the task! —Come, all my men; here goes the way.

(They go off to the right, at the back.)

DAGNY. Sigurd, Sigurd, this misdeed must thou hinder.

SIGURD (goes quickly to the door of the hut, and calls in). Up from the board, Ornulf; take vengeance on Kare the Peasant.

ORNULF (comes out, with the rest). Kare the Peasant—where is he?

SIGURD. He is making for Gunnar's hall to burn it over their heads.

ORNULF. Ha-ha—let him do as he will; so shall I be avenged on Gunnar and Hiordis, and afterwards I can deal with Kare.

SIGURD. Ay, that rede avails not; wouldst thou strike at Kare, thou must seek him out to-night; for when his misdeed is done, he will take to the mountains. I have challenged Gunnar to single combat; him thou hast safely enough, unless I myself—but no matter. — To-night he must be shielded from his foes; it would ill befit thee to let such a dastard as Kare rob thee of thy revenge.

ORNULF. Thou say'st truly. To-night will I shield the slayer of Thorolf; but to-morrow he must die.

SIGURD. He or I—doubt not of that!

ORNULF. Come then, to take vengeance for Ornulf's sons.

(He goes out with his men by the back, to the right.)

SIGURD. Dagny, do thou follow them; —I must bide here; for the rumour of the combat is already abroad, and I may not meet Gunnar ere the time comes. But thou—do thou keep rein on thy father; he must go honourably to work; in Gunnar's hall there are many women; no harm must befall Hiordis or the rest.

DAGNY. Yes, I will follow them. Thou hast a kind thought even for Hiordis; I thank thee.

SIGURD. Go, go, Dagny!

DAGNY. I go; but be thou at ease as to Hiordis; she has gilded armour in her bower, and will know how to shield herself.

SIGURD. That deem I too; but go thou nevertheless; guide thy father's course; watch over all—and over Gunnar's wife!

DAGNY. Trust to me. Farewell, till we meet again.

(She follows the others.)

SIGURD. 'Tis the first time, foster-brother, that I stand weaponless whilst thou art in danger. (Listens.) I hear shouts and sword-strokes; —they are already at the hall. (Goes towards the right, but stops and recoils in astonishment.) Hiordis! Comes she hither!

(HIORDIS enters, clad in a short scarlet kirtle, with gilded armour: helmet, hauberk, arm-plates, and greaves. Her hair is flying loose; at her back hangs a quiver, and at her belt a small shield. She has in her hand the bow strung with her hair.)

HIORDIS (hastily looking behind her, as though in dread of something pursuing her, goes close up to SIGURD, seizes him by the arm, and whispers:) Sigurd, Sigurd, canst thou see it?

SIGURD. What? Where ?

HIORDIS. The wolf there—close behind me; it does not move; it glares at me with its two red eyes. It is my wraith, [1], Sigurd! Three times has it appeared to me; that bodes that I shall surely die to-night!

[1] The word "wraith" is here used in an obviously inexact sense; but the wraith seemed to be the nearest equivalent in English mythology to the Scandinavian "fylgie, " an attendant spirit, often regarded as a sort of emanation from the person it accompanied, and sometimes (as in this case) typifying that person's moral attributes.

SIGURD. Hiordis, Hiordis!

HIORDIS. It has sunk into the earth! Yes, yes, now it has warned me.

SIGURD. Thou art sick; come, go in with me.

HIORDIS. Nay, here will I bide; I have but little time left.

SIGURD. What has befallen thee?

HIORDIS. What has befallen? That know I not; but true was it what thou said'st to-day, that Gunnar and Dagny stand between us; we must away from them and from life: then can we be together!

SIGURD. We? Ha, thou meanest— —!

HIORDIS (with dignity). I have been homeless in this world from that day thou didst take another to wife. That was ill done of thee! All good gifts may a man give his faithful friend—all, save the woman he loves; for if he do that, he rends the Norn's secret web, and two lives are wrecked. An unerring voice within me tells me I came into the world that my strong soul might cheer and sustain thee through heavy days, and that thou wast born to the end I might find in *one* man all that seemed to me great and noble; for this I know Sigurd—had we two held together, thou hadst become more famous than all others, and I happier.

SIGURD. It avails not now to mourn. Thinkest thou it is a merry life that awaits me? To be by Dagny's side day by day, and feign a love my heart shrinks from? Yet so it must be; it cannot be altered.

HIORDIS (in a growing frenzy). It *shall* be altered! We must out of this life, both of us! Seest thou this bow-string? With it can I surely hit my mark; for I have crooned fair sorceries over it! (Places an arrow in the bow, which is strung.) Hark! hearest thou that rushing in the air? It is the dead men's ride to Nalhal: I have bewitched them hither; —we two will join them in their ride!

SIGURD (shrinking back). Hiordis, Hiordis—I fear thee!

HIORDIS (not heeding him). Our fate no power can alter now! Oh, 'tis better so than if thou hadst wedded me here in this life—if I had sat in thy homestead weaving linen and wool for thee and bearing thee children—pah!

SIGURD. Hold, hold! Thy sorcery has been too strong for thee; thou art soul-sick, Hiordis! (Horror-struck.) Ha, see—see! Gunnar's hall—it is burning!

HIORDIS. Let it burn, let it burn! The cloud-hall up yonder is loftier than Gunnar's rafter-roof!

SIGURD. But Egil, thy son—they are slaying him!

HIORDIS. Let him die—my shame dies with him!

SIGURD. And Gunnar—they are taking thy husband's life!

HIORDIS. What care I! A better husband shall I follow home this night! Ay, Sigurd, so must it be; here on this earth is no happiness for me. The White God is coming northward; him will I not meet; the old gods are strong no longer; —they sleep, they sit half shadow-high; —with them will we strive! Out of this life, Sigurd; I will enthrone thee king in heaven, and I will sit at thy side. (The storm bursts wildly.) Hark, hark, here comes our company! Canst see the black steeds galloping? —one is for me and one for thee. (Draws the arrow to her ear and shoots.) Away, then, on thy last ride home!

SIGURD. Well aimed, Hiordis!

(He falls.)

HIORDIS (jubilant, rushes up to him). Sigurd, my brother, —now art thou mine at last!

SIGURD. Now less than ever. Here our ways part; for I am a Christian man.

HIORDIS (appalled). Thou——! Ha, no, no!

SIGURD. The White God is mine; King AEthelstan taught me to know him; it is to him I go.

HIORDIS (in despair). And I——! (Drops her bow.) Woe! woe!

SIGURD. Heavy has my life been from the hour I tore thee out of my own heart and gave thee to Gunnar. Thanks, Hiordis; —now am I so light and free.

(Dies.)

HIORDIS (quietly). Dead! Then truly have I brought my soul to wreck! (The storm increases; she breaks forth wildly.) They come! I have bewitched them hither! No, no! I will not go with you! I will not ride without Sigurd! It avails not—they see me; they laugh and beckon to me; they spur their horses! (Rushes out to the edge of the cliff at the back.) They are upon me; —and no shelter no hiding-place! Ay, mayhap at the bottom of the sea!

(She casts herself over.) (ORNULF, DAGNY, GUNNAR, with EGIL, followed by SIGURD'S and ORNULF'S men, gradually enter from the right.)

ORNULF (turning towards the grave-mound). Now may ye sleep in peace; for ye lie not unavenged.

DAGNY (entering). Father, father—I die of fear—all that bloody strife—and the storm; —hark, hark!

GUNNAR (carrying EGIL). Peace, and shelter for my child!

ORNULF. Gunnar!

GUNNAR. Ay, Ornulf, my homestead is burnt and my men are slain; I am in thy power; do with me what thou wilt!

ORNULF. That Sigurd must look to. But in, under roof! It is not safe out here.

DAGNY. Ay, in, in! (Goes towards the boat house, catches sight of SIGURD'S body, and shrieks.) Sigurd, my husband! —They have slain him! (Throwing herself upon him.)

ORNULF (rushes up). Sigurd!

GUNNAR (sets EGIL down). Sigurd dead!

DAGNY (looks despairingly at the men, who surround the body). No, no, it is not so; —he must be alive! (Catches sight of the bow.) Ha, what is that? (Rises.)

ORNULF. Daughter, it is as first thou saidst—Sigurd is slain.

GUNNAR (as if seized by a sudden thought). And Hiordis! —Has Hiordis been here?

DAGNY (softly and with self-control). I know not; but this I know, that her bow has been here.

GUNNAR. Ay, I thought as much!

DAGNY. Hush, hush! (To herself.) So bitterly did she hate him!

GUNNAR (aside). She has slain him—the night before the combat; then she loved me after all.

(A thrill of dread runs through the whole group; ASGARDSREIEN— the ride of the fallen heroes to Valhal—hurtles through the air.)

EGIL (in terror). Father! See, see!

GUNNAR. What is it?

EGIL. Up there—all the black horses— —!

GUNNAR. It is the clouds that— —

ORNULF. Nay, it is the dead men's home-faring.

EGIL (with a shriek). Mother is with them!

DAGNY. All good spirits!

GUNNAR. Child, what say'st thou?

EGIL. There—in front—on the black horse! Father, father!

(EGIL clings in terror to his father; a short pause; the storm passes over, the clouds part, the moon shines peacefully on the scene.)

GUNNAR (in quiet sorrow). Now is Hiordis surely dead!

ORNULF. So it must be, Gunnar; —and my vengeance was rather against her than thee. Dear has this meeting been to both of us; — — — — there is my hand; be there peace between us!

GUNNAR. Thanks, Ornulf! And now aboard; I sail with thee to Iceland.

ORNULF. Ay, to Iceland! Long will it be ere our forth-faring is forgotten.

> Weapon wielding warrior's meeting,
> woeful by the northern seaboard,
> still shall live in song and saga
> while our stem endure in Iceland.